MY BEAUTIFUL AMEN

By Angelina A Amedeka

THE BOOK CHIEF®

IGNITE YOUR WRITING

Published by The Book Chief Publishing House 2024
Suite 2A, Blackthorn House, St Paul's Square, Birmingham, B3 1RL
www.thebookchief.com

ISBN: 978-1-0686981-6-3

Book Cover Design: Deearo Marketing
Editor: Laura Billingham
Typesetting: Nicola Matthews
Publishing: Sharon Brown

Published by The Book Chief Publishing House

Table of Contents

4

To God

Acknowledgements

I would like to acknowledge those who prayed with me and supported me financially as I wrote the story of my life. I thank you for your impact and motivation.

God (Alpha and Omega)

Reverend Alfred Nartey Accam (husband)

Bishop SN Mensah (FGCI)

Bishop Dela Edudzie Fiagome (FGCI)

Reverend Fred Abeka (FGCI)

Reverend Afrani

Reverend Isaac Popolampo

Pastor Godwin Asem

Elder Frank

Fred Borson

Mr and Mrs Ohene

Godwin Avorduagu

Antuanette Avorduagu

Mosses Agbemabiawo

Petrona Sewell Dawkins

Deborah Nartey Amedeka

Victoria Nartey Amedeka

Eli Nartey Amedeka

Introduction

Follow His Light

The Lord himself goes before you and will be with you; he will never leave you nor forsake you. Do not be afraid; do not be discouraged.

Deuteronomy 31:8

From the beginning of my life, I have been a warrior, right from my mother's womb, amid the turmoil of famine and military unrest in Ghana, and during the depths of bereavement, and every time, God has protected me as I journeyed through the pain.

I am only 49 years old, but my life has already been intricate and varied, taking me from my birth country of Ghana in West Africa to Spain, where I hold citizenship, and now to the UK, where I live with my husband and three beautiful children.

I am writing this book because I would like my story to have an impact; I would like my life to encourage and inspire people while putting a smile on their faces. My mum always tried to empower, advise and motivate me to do something positive with my future, to help both myself and others. This book is also written in her memory to let her know how proud I am of her, and to leave a legacy in her name. I have been through so much in my life and rather than keeping these experiences to myself, I want to use them to help others see that there is hope in every situation. Every success in my life has been a battle, and I use hope and strength to secure my road to victory. I always smile and treat people with love, so it can seem that I do not have problems, but you will be surprised at the challenges I have faced and yet, I am still standing, still strong and still trusting in God.

Life is a journey, and on your way, you will meet many obstacles, potholes and curves. A motorway might direct you straight ahead, but before long, you will reach an exit. This does not mean you should stop when you come to a traffic light, or go back; instead, you should try to move on. In my life, I have learnt to enjoy the challenges I have encountered, and I have learnt to keep moving forwards in many different ways.

God has demonstrated His immeasurable love to me in special ways by sending people into my life for a reason and connecting me to those are helpful. I came into this world with nothing, but He has guided me in my darkest moments, enabling me to see His light and take strength from adversity, teaching me that before you can give a testimony, you must first go through a test.

I was inspired to write this book by the Very Reverend Bishop SN Mensah of the Full Gospel Church International, whose words always challenge me to do something meaningful. He encourages us to be proactive with ourselves and to impart what we have learnt in this life by leaving a legacy. He reminds us that while it is good to wait as a Christian, you cannot sit in your home praying for change, or that a job will fall in front of you. While praying, you must go online, research, go to the job centre and make a move, and then, by God's grace and your faith, the job or the change will occur. We must not to be lazy Christians; instead, we must be ready to make the first move.

I was also inspired by Reverend Fred Abeka, who prophesied on my graduation day that I would write a book and that many books will come from me. I prayed about his prophecy and took the step to fulfil the spoken word of God.

So is my word that goes out from my mouth:
It will not return to me empty,
but will accomplish what I desire
and achieve the purpose for which I sent it.

Isaiah 55:11

PART ONE

Life In Ghana Before Marriage

Chapter 1

A Precious Daughter

Once upon a time, there was a beautiful Ghanaian twin princess called Regina, whose middle name was Atsufi. According to tradition, the female twin takes the name Atsufi, and the male Atu.

This beautiful princess was my mum.

As we all know, mums are special, and I am very attached to mine, for I shared an exceptionally close bond with her. Regina Atsufi Agbemabiawo was a strong, funny and caring woman, dedicated to her friends and family. She loved me very much and I loved her; we chatted and communicated like close friends, a big sister with her kid sister in tow.

She sacrificed so much to facilitate my return to school, which reflects how passionate and committed she was to my education. She often told me there were things she was unable to achieve and that I should try everything possible to strive forward. She took care of many people, adopting children and always being a humorous conversationalist, earning her the nickname Daadra, which means 'kid sister' in Ewe. In times of trouble, when I was younger, she sang songs to help soothe me:

Do not be afraid,

as God is your backbone,

and no matter what the storm looks like,

there will always be peace.

Another song that reminds me of her is,

With Jesus in the boat I can

smile at the storm when I am sailing home.

This she sang to reassure us that, with Jesus close by, everything will be fine and peaceful, and we will always overcome (Mark 4:35–41).

Regina advised me to be respectful and kind, which helped me grow up obediently, with an intuitive love for people. Using her guidance, I can see this seed growing in my children when I teach them how to approach people and to demonstrate their love. Wherever she is in the world, her spirit will be at peace, and I hope she is as proud of me as I am of her.

My mum, Regina

My mum was born on 20th July 1933 and was her parents' sixth child.

Despite having a twin brother, she was very close to her elder sister AblaviDC Agbemabiawo, with whom she shared a twin-like bond.

Regina attended a Roman Catholic primary school from 1943 to 1950 under Renown Teachers. After finishing middle school, she went to a vocational school in the coastal town of Keta, where, upon graduation, she established herself as a sewing teacher. Regina was very talented and derived much enjoyment from her time as a seamstress, producing garments such as choir robes and suits for men and women, as well as sharing her skills with others. However, in the 1970s, she was forced to make the difficult decision to leave her village and relocate to Accra Tema Newtown in order to support AblaviDC's flourishing fishing business. She found the time very challenging because she loved her job, but AblaviDC had bought two big fishing boats and needed extra hands to help. The port was always full of pallets of fish arriving off the boats, and AblaviDC would be standing there with her fish, shouting "Awelewele", which means "Come and pick it!" This earnt her the nickname Awelewele!

Regina began buying the fish her sister caught on the coast and transporting it to different cities and towns; if prices were low, she took the catch of fish to the cold store warehouse to store it until its value increased. One day, a shortage of fish meant she had to look elsewhere for her supply, so she approached the State Fishing Corporation, one of the biggest cold stores in Ghana, where food was stored in refrigerated buildings. This was where my dad, Alfred Amedeka, first spotted her.

Two lives collide

My dad was the company's marketing manager. A quiet man, he had worked for the State Fishing Corporation since 1957 in a position that saw him travel east of the capital to the coastal city of Tema, as well as to Koforidua, Kumasi, Ho, Hohoe and Accra itself. During his time there, people called him the 'money man' because he controlled the company's finances, making significant sums of money. Born in 1925 in southeast Ghana, my dad grew up in a town called Weta in the Volta Region, before going to elementary school, college and university, where he studied marketing. He then went on to become a lecturer at a university in Accra.

After their first meeting, my parents got to know each other better, and before long, Alfred called my mum's family to ask for her hand in marriage. Previously, my mum was married to a man called Lawrence Akpalu, who was the dad of my elder brother, Mr Franklin Atsigui Akpalu; I was told it was a wonderful union, but, owing to another love story, it did not succeed. Lawrence was already married when he met my mum, and while he did not live with his wife, she heard about his new relationship after her friend attended a large party to celebrate Franklin's birth. Shortly afterwards, Lawrence's wife turned up at the village and said, "I am back to take what belongs to me. You have stolen my husband. You must pack your things and leave."

My mum is a calm person who does not like trouble, so she went to visit her grandmother and decided not to go back to her husband. Lawrence kept begging her to return, but Regina felt threatened by his wife, could not stand the fight and could sense danger ahead. Sometimes in life, you need to learn to fight for what is important, but in this case, my mum was forced to give up. After her first marriage broke down, Regina decided not to marry again to avoid having children with different fathers, something that she felt could ruin her reputation. This, according to her, led my dad to be very, very persistent with his proposal, but, finally, she accepted. Always dressed in a suit, my dad was a very handsome, irresistible man; he did not

18

expect women to say no to him. They fell deeply for one another, and I was the fruit of this love.

A miraculous arrival

When she was pregnant with me, my mum moved back to the village of Tegbi in the Volta Region, where she had grown up. There, with the support of her family, she restarted the sewing business she had loved and set up shop in a wooden building. One day, when she was eight months' pregnant and working in her shop, a huge storm blew up which suddenly lifted the building from the ground. My mum was terrified and wondered what was happening, but before she knew it, the wind took her (and me, in her belly) up with the shop. As it hung in the air, she cried and screamed, but everyone else in the village was sheltering inside their homes and could not hear her over the noise of the storm, so she began to pray. She asked God how she would survive and prayed for him to provide protection. As she did so, the shop dropped suddenly to the ground, landing her on a bush. She saw that the Lord was with her and knew she was safe. My mum then started feeling early contractions and, finding herself unable to walk, she crawled out of her shop, and screamed for someone to come to her aid, but Tegbi was a small village with no ambulances, which made finding help for her very challenging. She was carried to the roadside by local men, where a car finally took her to Keta General Government Hospital.

By the time my mum arrived at the hospital, the situation was complicated and precarious because I had moved, making it difficult for the doctors to help with my delivery. They faced a scenario in which either my mum survived and I died, or I survived and she did not, but God knew me since I was a clot of blood and he predestined my arrival.

Regina called on her faith and prayed to God that he would help her through this challenge and that she would not lose me. The Bible says, in the Book of Proverbs, that the hope of the righteous shall never be cut off, and that we are born and created in a special form and for a purpose. In Ecclesiastes, the Bible says that "Whatsoever exists has already been named" (6:10) and so, finally, on a beautiful Tuesday afternoon, 10th July 1973, I was delivered safely into this world.

A broken family

My mum was very happy to have me; my dad, however, had desperately wanted a son and he was disappointed at having a daughter, abandoning my mum shortly after visiting me for the first time. He went on to have children with seven women – the result of his persistent search for male offspring – all of them fair in complexion. Out of my stepsiblings, the eldest is female, followed by a male and then female. He finally settled with the seventh woman, Janet, my stepmum.

My dad retired from the State Fishing Corporation in 1981, redirecting his attention to rice cultivation and buying lots of land in a town called Afife in the Volta Region, as well as in Weija in the Greater Accra Region. He was a very hard worker, and as well as supplying rice for the people of Ghana, he grew an impressive property portfolio by building houses and a petrol station.

At that time, he wasn't a Christian, but by 1987, he had accepted Christ and committed himself fully to the Lord. He became quite a strict Christian, and my siblings and I felt that impact when he introduced the Word of God to us. He made sure we dressed modestly – we dared not wear short clothes in his house – and he asked us not to watch television. He called the television the 'devil box' because he feared it would pollute our minds and take us into darkness. Sometimes, we laughed at him because when wrestling matches were broadcast, he would put on the television, cross his legs and watch it intently. Similarly, we remember him fondly when it was time for the news as he loved to listen to world events.

Chapter 2

Very Loved

I grew up in Tegbi until I was six years old, when Regina decided to go back to Accra Tema because she wanted to raise me in a city. I remember being carried by my mum in those days and feeling very loved; according to family members, I never cried, was a joyful child, and did not trouble my mum until I grew up and was a bit more stubborn. My mum always wanted the best for me, sending me to a private school called Compresco Academy, and encouraging me, as her only daughter, to study hard.

I was so happy to start school; it was something I had wished for while growing up in the village. I watched the other children, all of them dressed in their uniforms, going to school in the morning and I would ask my mum when I could go. She reassured me that as soon as we moved to the city, she would register me at school, and this made me so happy. Regina prepared everything for me, including buying me a school desk, which is something you would not need to do in the UK. I have happy memories of carrying my books to school and my mum following me with my bags.

When I was 10 years old, my mum told me stories about her life and how, among all her sisters, she was the only one who went to school, along with her brother. The rest of the family worked in the fishing business, but she always insisted on the importance of a good education, and I, naturally, learnt to share this ideology. From a young age, I loved the idea of school and pretended I was a teacher, telling my friends that they were my students and they needed to listen to me. People called me 'Teacher', and if I go back to that area of Ghana, some people still know me by this name.

Christian roots

I was born into a Roman Catholic family and baptised as a baby. As a child I followed this faith and joined the Catholic Youth Organisation (CYO), which is a bit like Scouts, going on camping trips, wearing a unique green and white uniform with a scarf around my neck and a hat; it was beautiful. My siblings went to a Pentecostal church, which was where my dad repented and became a strict Christian. When I joined his church, I was required to do certain things, such as wearing conservative clothes and attending early morning services, and I saw profound differences in the way each church operated.

Roman Catholic services had a rehearsed, familiar structure in which prayers were read and repeated, and certain scriptures were anticipated at specific times, whereas at the Pentecostal church, devotion was more energetic and involved reading the Bible, and talking about Jesus Christ and the miracles he performed; it was a completely different world.

I started having an interest in the teachings of and the testimonies about Lord Jesus Christ and my family would ask me to pray, but I did not know how to do this and felt shy.

I realised something was wrong and decided to offer to help teach children at their Sunday school. The experience soaked me in this world, and I started believing certain things about God and Jesus Christ. Christianity is a form of education, and the more you study the Word, the more you know why you are a Christian and where Christianity is leading you. I have witnessed so many miracles in my life that Jesus did for me personally, saving me from the hands of soldiers during the 1981 famine and sparing my mum and I from a barrage of bullets, that they make me believe in God. Many people died, but we were saved, and my life is testimony to a miraculous God, which is why I have named this book My Beautiful Amen. It signifies the affirmation of my prayer. It means to me that surely this battle will be over. And truly, God will prove himself faithful, and so shall it be. With Jesus in my boat, I can smite at the storm.

The Bible says, "We should call on him and he will answer us and show us great and mighty things that we do not know" (Jeremiah 33:3). Any time I call on God and say my Beautiful Amen, he responds to me in one way or another, even if it takes time. It is like a child asking their parents to do something for them; we need to obey and wait patiently, and we should not put pressure on God.

Power through song

Music sustained me in my childhood and into adulthood, acting as one of my strongest weapons during personal battles. I love music so much and use it to worship and praise God, in the same way that it is used in the Bible, when a group that is outnumbered by its enemy joins together in song while sheltering from an attack behind a closed door. The people sing and praise to God until it is safe to emerge, whereupon they discover the battle has already been won; the enemy has destroyed itself by fighting internally and many of them are now dead (King Jehoshaphat 2, Chronicles 20:17–22). This shows us that there is power in worship, and if you worship diligently and form a fellowship, you will see the manifestation of God in your life.

The Bible shows this power to us again in the story of Paul and Silas (Acts 16–34), in which two men imprisoned for preaching the gospel refuse to stop worshipping, bravely continuing to sing and praise God in the prison yard. Then, one day, lo and behold, a heavily fortified prison door that is guarded and weighed down by locks and chains opens, and they are free to escape. God performs a miracle and shows us that when you have no hope and no one to turn to, he will send people on your behalf.

This intimate relationship with God is very powerful and I always use worship and song as a weapon in the battles I face to encourage myself forwards.

> I'm fighting a battle,
> you've already won.
> No matter what comes my way,
> I will overcome.
> I know what you're doing,
> and I know what you've done.
> I'm fighting a battle,
> you've already won.

I am also motivated by the song *One thing I know, God will work it out*. It alerts me to the fact that God is there and has not forgotten about me. The beginning of the song tells me that no matter what challenges come my way, he will work it out:

Before I knew my name,
before I was truly formed,
he was making way for me.

Chapter 3

God Will Provide

In 1983, a shortage of rain and widespread crop failures over the preceding two years led to a severe and terrible famine in Ghana. I remember this time so well; it was very tough. I didn't suffer severe hunger because we were lucky enough to have money, but food was so scarce that we were unable to buy much. Tragedy was visible at every corner, with streams and rivers dried up, and farms burnt by bush fires.

It was sometimes possible to buy rice and corn from food smugglers, so when we heard that a smuggler's ship with food aboard had docked at the main harbour in Tema, it was an opportunity to see if they would sell anything to us. The atmosphere was very tense at the time and, with soldiers patrolling and all the smugglers in the area, also dangerous. If the soldiers got hold of you, they would either throw you into the sea, pack you in a lorry and dump you somewhere, or punish you severely.

Although I was only 10 years old, my mum said I could join a group of people going down to the port, hoping I would come back home with something to eat. This was not an easy decision for my mum, but as I was the youngest in the group, the others promised to take care of me. I was able to buy some rice, but as we left the main entrance of the harbour, we heard soldiers fire a warning shot. I remember running and running and having to climb up a tall hill while praying and asking God for protection. This is the beautiful prayer I said as I cried and ran:

> Please God, have mercy on me. God, you are our refuge in times of trouble. Lord, please. You said you are my strength, and you will be ever present in times of trouble, please, this is the time. Lord – save me.

Then, before I knew it, I found myself somewhere safe, still running and tightly clutching my rice. The people I had been with had all scattered and run for their lives, so I was alone, with nobody around me. I wondered what would happen to me if the soldiers came after me, but I trusted in God and kept walking for a very long time. I saw a company I recognised, Cement Wares, which was well known, and I was then able to follow a familiar bus route home. My mum was devastated when she saw the incident on the news, and very happy to see me when I arrived home safely. Afterwards, I heard that some in our group had been caught, and we did not know if they were alive or not, so I thanked God for my life.

The famine also forced many Ghanaians to travel to Nigeria, but they were quickly ejected by the Nigerian government, which did not want migrants settling in their country. Ghanaian travellers would often return to Ghana with their belongings zipped into distinctive check-patterned bags that became known as 'Ghana Must Go' bags. The Nigerian president Alhaji Shehu Shagari wanted Ghanaians to take absolutely everything they owned back to Ghana with them, leaving nothing behind. I have since watched a number of his videos on social media, all of them characterised by bold demands that all Ghanaians leave the country. The Nigerians made large sums of money selling these bags to Ghanaians because everyone needed several of them in order to carry their belongings home. It was a very bad time.

My mum and I lived on the coast, very close to the sea in Tema, and we sometimes saw the ships that brought the Ghanaian migrants back to Ghana. We would stand at the seashore, crying as we watched them, for we could tell that the ships were overloaded and could not move properly. People were packed in like sardines, and you could see those who could not bear it throwing themselves into the sea. We heard on the news of shipwrecks and of the people who did not survive the journey. As children, we saw dead bodies lying on the shore. I remember seeing them with my naked eye. Such things should not be witnessed by a child.

It was very sad, and it left me, as a young child, feeling scared and worried that something might happen to me. I did not understand fully what was happening, or have a clue why such things were happening, but since then, some of the Ghanaians who returned from Nigeria have started sharing their stories about the events they suffered. Some women talked of having to give themselves to Nigerian men in order to obtain food; they went through so much. We saw wickedness dominate the land and it was so devastating. Ghana has incredible resources – gold, diamonds and oil – but our leaders have not helped us at all; they have been selfish and incompetent, and the country has suffered great poverty and suffering.

Food in a time of famine

As Christians, we are taught not to worry about what to eat or wear, and not to worry about tomorrow, for tomorrow will worry for itself. The word of God says, "Behold the fowls of the air: for they sow not, neither do they reap, nor gather into barns; yet your heavenly Father feedeth them" (Matthew 6:26).

Being unable to buy food was very tough. We were forced to live on substances such as kanzo, the starchy crust produced when you cook rice over a flame. People were so desperate they started selling and living off the crust of a food called banku shishi, which was made by mixing corn dough with water until it turned solid. We invented a type of fast food by hooking two empty tuna tins together over a fire, putting corn into one of them and then spinning it repeatedly until the corn was roasted and ready to eat. It became a real trend, with groups of young people sitting around fires spinning sets of tuna tins. We also ate a mixture of corn and peanuts known as ableke nkatia, and gari (a creamy granular flour) and coconut. There were always queues for food and my mum and I would wait for long periods of time to collect bread or rice before taking it home. I felt bad as a child and did not understand everything, but one thing that was on my side was that my family had money, so I did not experience severe hunger. Even if food was expensive, my mum would risk her life to get it for me, but some people were not so lucky, and some died.

The good thing about the whole story was that God sent help through a group of European Christians who had heard about Ghana's famine and wanted to help the entire country. They saved the situation by bringing ships full of rice, corn and bread, which they distributed to the churches, where Christians and people of different faiths could queue for the food. Hallelujah! We all smiled and felt that God had saved us by providing for us. The missionaries understood that some families could not even afford to buy cooking utensils, so some of them cooked the food and told people to simply bring their containers.

We still went to school, but it was very difficult; some children did not even have shoes and came to school barefoot. I felt pity for them, and because I loved giving, I sometimes took a bag of rice for a friend at school. My mum loved giving too, so she never stopped me. To me, the joy of giving is something I have felt since infancy; it is like a passion and a God-given gift. During my time at school, if I did not have enough money to buy a Christmas card, I would create or design one instead. I am very creative and would paint some card, fold it nicely and then give it to somebody, or buy some chocolates and gift them. I believe my love for giving is in my bloodline, an inherited trait and one that I saw in my mum as clearly as she saw it in her own. She would often describe how my grandmother, Madam Sexovor Galedzi Kokoroko, would entertain a house full of people nearly every day, feeding them, letting some of them sleep and generally looking after them before they went home. I share this love of organising people and of putting a smile on their faces by inviting them into my home and cooking for them, whether they are from Ghana, or Spain, or elsewhere.

A coup d'état

In 1981, a political coup d'état was started in Ghana by former President JJ Rawlings, a military man who sacrificed himself in order to try to end widespread hardship and corruption in the country. A 6 o'clock curfew was introduced, but one day, as my mum and I walked home, there was so much traffic that we knew we would not get back in time. There were helicopters all around us and gunshots being fired, so my mum covered me with a cloth to protect me.

It was completely dark and I could not see a thing; I was scared and felt certain I would not survive. Gunshots sounded loudly all around us and bullets rained down from the helicopters above. I knew how dangerous the situation was and how easily I could be hit by a bullet. People often died from hunger in their own homes because they were too afraid to go outside, and some died of shock. I thought to myself that this could be the end of my mum and me, but she kept protecting me. We hid between the houses until the helicopters passed over and then we would set off again, stopping and starting, until we made it home.

I asked myself, "What kind of world is this? When is this going to be over?" My whole world felt so agitated and I did not know what to do. I asked my mum if we would survive, and she reassured me that we would and began to share her story about what she went through when she gave birth to me, telling me how God saved her. She told me not to worry, that God was with us. She gave me the extra name 'Mawulawoe', which means 'God will provide', to symbolise the challenges we had overcome together right from the moment I was born, and to encourage and empower me. She kept telling me not to worry, but I was scared and reminded her that people were being hit by bullets every day and were dying like chickens on the streets. This experience stopped me from going to school until Rawlings began to win the battle and regain stability, and things became calmer.

At that time, people thought Rawlings was wrong to use military force and to kill people, but now, the country is in such a terrible state that Ghanaians wish he could come back and take over again. Rawlings died in 2020, but he remains one of Ghana's political heroes, highly respected for the degree of stability he restored by 1984, which led many to believe he did his job well.

The power of prayer

Ghana is a Christian and Muslim country where people collectively believe in the power of prayer, and the events of 1983 remind me of the story of Moses (Exodus 2:1–10). Moses' mother defies the Pharaoh's orders that all first-born males must be killed and hides her son among the reeds by the side of the Nile River, where he is found by the Pharaoh's daughter and raised in the leader's house. Once grown to manhood, Moses rescues the Israelites from slavery and experiences the pressures of being a leader, especially during his people's 40 days in the wilderness, where there is no food, and his followers wonder if they should return to Egypt.

Moses prays to God and food begins to fall like rain from the sky, prompting people to run with their baskets to benefit from this miracle. Shortly afterwards, they find themselves at the edge of the Red Sea, terrified and with nowhere to flee as the Pharaoh's soldiers close on them, Moses prays to God to help him again – and God shows up again. This time, God says to Moses, "Hit the water with your stick and the sea will divide in two." Moses obeys and all his followers pass through the sea safely, and despite being hounded by soldiers, Moses continues to believe in God's protection and behaves courageously throughout.

In life's challenging situations, we must sometimes stop and discover this type of courage so that we can find a way to push on through. I am grateful that I knew God from an early age as this has helped me very much, and without my faith, I do not know if I would be where I am today. I think back to myself as a little, young child running up and down the market stalls, doing the household chores alongside my education while thinking about my mum, who lived alone. Through all those challenges,

I kept telling myself, "I will not be like this for ever – one day I will become somebody." I often felt like crying when I was growing up, but I kept some hope that things would be well. I soon realised that God has a plan and has kept me alive for a purpose. The Bible says, "The secret things belong to Him alone" (Deuteronomy 29:29) so we cannot question God; He is the Alpha and Omega and the creator of the whole universe.

Chapter 4

Seeking an Education

I returned to school in 1991, but Regina felt our village was too remote and encouraged me to live with my dad in Accra Tema Community 10 in the capital. Although she was still upset with him for leaving her when I was born, he was one of the richest men in Ghana and my mum felt I would have better opportunities if I stayed with him. His wealth was something I was aware of as a child, especially when my stepmum, Janet Amoafo, showed me stacks of money stored inside his wardrobe. My mum was also concerned that some of my school friends had fallen pregnant and she did not want me facing such a fate.

I was unsure about the move at first as it meant leaving her behind at a time when I was the only one living with her and taking care of her. We had also spent so much time together in my early childhood that leaving her was a very tough decision to take. However, she insisted and described it as the best sacrifice she could make, and one that would give me the most promising future. I thought about her reasons and agreed that I did not want the same life as the young girls in my village.

Janet, my dad's wife, was a woman I grew to really love, so I left with a heavy heart and, promising to visit my mother every weekend, went to live with my dad and stepmum.

I was about 13 years old when I moved to Community 10 to continue with my education. My peers and I were the first batch of children to start junior secondary school, which the government had just established. The fledgling nature of this educational system meant we struggled a lot of the time because it was not well organised or planned, but, thank God, I did well. I was very smart and enjoyed drawing and creating things in art, and, although I found maths and science challenging, I completed junior school with distinction.

Once I started high school, our curriculum became very mixed up and we found ourselves doing 12 subjects at a time, which was very intense and confusing. When my year group finished in 1993, none of us did particularly well and it was the talk of the town; everyone was complaining about the new system. The majority of the year ended up doing different things, but despite failing one of my exams, I was willing to carry on in education. However, living with my stepsiblings, Janet and my dad, meant there were many different opinions and influences in the house, which left me confused.

A house of plenty

My dad built our family home on a large plot of land, which he bought and cultivated, surrounding the house with an abundance of trees. He loved doing something for himself, and gardening and farming became his hobby; he was always busy and enterprising during his retirement. In his garden, he planted coconut, cashew, mango and palm trees, as well as peanuts, beans and corn, while nurturing his livestock. Every season, he grew something new, and while we never helped him cultivate the crops, we were always the first to eat them.

During those days, my siblings and I would climb the cashew nut trees, prodding the fruits and eating the nuts in the hot African sun, before returning to ground level to play our traditional childhood games. This period of my life was wonderful, and I was exceptionally grateful to God for providing such beauty.

Six yellow coconut trees stood in front of the house; these trees were particularly special to my dad, and he warned us regularly that we must not touch them. He would harvest a huge number of coconuts and either give them to his friends or sell them. As children, we wore wide smiles whenever he left the house, watching as he stood in front of the main gates and lifted his head to slowly count the coconuts. Once he was out of sight, my siblings would rush to the trees, climb them, shake them vigorously, drink the milk from the coconuts they shook down, and then tidy everything away before he returned. He began to notice that coconuts were missing and asked us if we were taking them. "OK, we shall see," he said, when we denied any involvement. "We shall see the mouse that is in this house."

The day came that my dad left home as usual, but instead of his familiar routine, he went secretly to our neighbour's house opposite in the hope of returning to catch us in the act. As soon as he was gone, my brothers climbed the trees, but by the time we had all sat down to enjoy the coconuts, our dad appeared, saying, "Aha – so you're the ones who've been taking them!" We all laughed, sharing this special moment.

A demanding dad

Away from the distractions of the garden, my dad was very strict, and we would be in a lot of trouble if we did not obey his instructions.

He felt strongly about propriety when it came to a man and a woman spending time together, especially once he became a born-again Christian. He insisted that we should never take a member of the opposite sex into our bedroom, but on the day my brother broke this rule, Dad barged in and pulled the girl from the house, leaving my brother angry and the girl deeply embarrassed. My dad also once took a big heavy stick to one of my sisters to discipline her because somebody had visited her. He never laid a hand on me, and, despite his strictness, I loved him.

Later in my life, when I was married and due to travel to Spain, he said he wanted to do something for me that he had never done to any of his children. He asked me to kneel at his feet, and he poured his blessings on me. It was the most overwhelming moment of my life, an experience I had never before encountered and one that was completely unexpected. I shed tears while he empowered me with his faith and prayers and made me feel special. He said I had been a good child and he admired the way I coped and stood firm, before counselling me to go to my husband. This act left me truly satisfied and gave me something I am so grateful for. It was worth more than any inheritance and felt like a crown being bestowed on me, a divine blessing.

Our fathers represent God and if your father blesses you, you experience the mighty hands of God. He speaks through women too, but men are the head of the family and represent God in this life. I have always been humble, and this has led God to shine his light on me. This can cause people to wish to bring me down; however, whatever falls down, will always spring back up, and as long as I have hope in God, I will endure and will be lifted up.

Sometimes, life is not comfortable, but hope will sustain you in whatever you are waiting for if you are determined, work hard and wait patiently.

Janet and Topsy

Janet was always very kind, and each time she returned from trips to London she brought gifts to share. She is a very neat person who takes pride in her surroundings, and she always ensured the compound was clean and tidy. My love of flowers comes from watching her tend to the garden, watering the beds and uprooting any dead plants.

Her dog Topsy was never far away and he became the family's guard dog, twice saving us from armed robbers and always making us feel safe and secure. I had never understood how attached some humans can become to their animals until I met Topsy and saw his devotion and ability to communicate; I loved him deeply.

My dad ran a shop at the front of the house which sold building materials. On one occasion, we had extra stock that needed to be stored inside the house before being packed. Topsy woke us at dawn, barking furiously, but at first my dad could not see anything. Topsy continued to bark, running to the gate in hot pursuit of robbers just as Dad caught sight of them jumping over the wall. Without Topsy, everything from the house would have been stolen and since then, we have never joked about him – he was our security. One day, unfortunately, while chasing a passer-by, he ran into the road, where he was hit by a car and his leg was broken. We cried for him and he reciprocated, with tears rolling from his eyes. His leg had to be amputated, but despite having only three and a half legs, he remained our strong protector and we all adored him.

Chapter 5

A Village at Play

During our childhood, we played many interesting and memorable games, some of which were particularly special. Each day, we organised our time and planned to do different things, such as play football, for which we made a ball by stuffing a sock with plastic things until it had a round shape and then sewing it shut. There was always someone knocking at my door to ask me to play. We did not even think about food when we played; even when our parents called to us to "Come and eat!" we continued playing. It was very peaceful, especially in the evening after 4 o'clock, when the sky turned a beautiful yellow, the moon began to appear and there was a lovely breeze.

Pilolo

Pilolo is similar to hide and seek, but in this game, a stick is hidden and has to be found. We would gather excitedly and wait until the child hiding the stick shouted "*Pilolo*." We would then all respond, "*Yafo be me*," which means "there is no crying in this game," but most of the time, the game ended in tears when one child took the lead after finding the stick, or if another took it from them. There was always lots of crying. The rules of the game were that when a child found the stick, they had to run as fast as they could to hand it back to the child who hid it before anyone else took it away. Everybody is after the same stick, so you had to be very fast or you would lose the game. Depending on how well hidden the stick was, a game could last for over half an hour, but once a child found and returned the stick, we then began the next round.

Throughout the game, you would hear choruses of "*Pilolo yafo be me*," and the more children were involved, the louder it sounded. We searched everywhere, digging down into the ground or turning the house upside down. Our parents could not understand and would exclaim, "Why, why all this?" We were children, so we did not care. We were excited and anxious to get hold of that stick. Occasionally, the stick would be impossible to find and we would start throwing things because we were so annoyed, which was when we would be in trouble with the stricter parents.

Once, a girl hid behind the door of her parents' bedroom and we all followed her inside until her mum saw us, and even though she knew we were playing, she screamed, "Come out of there!" I also remember very clearly the time I threw things around in a friend's house; his mother was so mad when she came home that she warned us not to visit her house again. Her son loved the game, and whenever we were back from school, he passed by our house, whispering to let us know he was there, and we would all rush outside.

Looking back and thinking about the game gives me a great feeling, and it was an activity we loved so much that I am thrilled by the memory of it. I experienced being the leader, and while I did not always win, I enjoyed strategising with my friends about where the stick could be and exploring every inch of where we played. Having taught it to my children here in the UK, I now realise how challenging the environment was in Ghana, with its big spaces and long paths; we always came back home very tired, whereas my children could only run from room to room.

Osungeli

In a game of *Osungeli*, we all lined up with home-made kites, watching them rise into the air, while spinning the string to encourage them to fly higher. Some children were very skilled at designing their kites and, colouring them red, gold and green, would make them resemble the Ghanaian flag. If their kites were particularly well built and beautiful, they would sell them for a few coins. We stood for hours measuring whose was the highest and feeling so good and happy as we looked on in wonder. I used to think of my kite as an aeroplane flying in the air, and it felt very special.

Our kites were made from the branches of large palm leaves, like those used to fashion brooms in Africa. We tore off the leaves and joined the wood together with rope, tied plastic sheets over the top to help the kite fly and attached long pieces of string, which we teased out in order to race our kites against one another.

One day, we played the game near the coast where the breeze helped the kites fly higher. We wanted to see whose kite would fly the highest. During the race, mine tore and became tangled in the kite of a boy called Kwame, who was next to me. We ran after the kites to search for them, screaming, "*Osungeli, osungeli!*" This happened again on another occasion, and this time Kwame started crying and told his mum, who took it very seriously. She came running after me, and, determined to get hold of me to beat me, she chased me for a long time. I was surprised and shocked and ran like never before until I reached somebody's house, unable to breathe, and told them what had

45

happened. The woman hid me for a couple of hours, and I then found my way home to tell my mum about the situation; it then became her problem too. My mum also took it seriously and confronted the other mum, telling her, "You cannot do this to my daughter." The two women did not talk for a long time.

Tumatu

To play *Tumatu*, we drew lines on the floor and numbered them, jumping between the lines while clapping and singing. We were always together, a mix of boys and girls of varying ages and from different schools, all having a wonderful time playing energetic activities outside. We became very close, and I miss many of the children I played with then, but I do not know how to find them. Nowadays, in a time of social media, when children do not seem to have time for such things, I see that this type of play no longer exists.

Mama na Papa

Mama na Papa was a role-playing game in which we pretended to run our own households. We asked our parents for our very own coal pots to put the charcoal in, or we would invent them and gather outside together to create a home. Sometimes we visited the outdoor market, known as *Abobosu*, in search of vegetables, and some store holders were kind enough to give us free food, or we could take a basket full of fruit and vegetables that were past their best. I remember putting onions,

tomatoes and okra in a plastic bag to carry back to our 'home', where we built a proper fire. Once lit, we used tuna tins as cooking pots and, as we did not have a fan, blew repeatedly on the flames.

We made proper soup, tasting it before serving portions to our make-believe husbands and children, and then we got ready to go out to an event. Sometimes children would say they were beaten when trying to pick up ingredients at the market, but as I always asked, I never experienced this. They were good times.

The only food we struggled to get from the market was fish, but interestingly, there was a beach close to us, and when the tide was out and the sea calm, we were able to catch fish or crabs. We lowered baskets into rock pools and once the small fish swam in, we quickly lifted them out. Our parents said they were not good for us, but we made soup out of them, and other Ghanaian dishes such as fufu, which is made by cooking and pounding cassava, and rounding it into balls ready for a soup or fish stew. We prepared the cassava in a wooden structure, not dissimilar to a pestle and mortar, copying the technique our parents used when pounding the vegetable. Fufu is still cooked in the UK, but technology means we can buy cassava or plantain powder and add it to boiling water until it forms the dough. It would also not be very sociable to pound cassava in the UK as it would disturb your neighbours, whereas back home in Ghana everyone is aware of it and it does not bother anyone.

I loved the cooking part of these games and encouraged my friends to visit the market by saying, "Hurry up! It's getting late." I grew up loving any cooking environment – it is in my blood – and I was lucky enough to be trained by my parents, my aunties and my stepmum, all of whom taught me so much.

Ampe

Ampe is a famous Ghanaian game in which a player tries to copy exactly the same movements at exactly the same time as their opponent, such as jumping in the air, waving their right arm and then clapping their hands together. Points are lost when the player misjudges, such as kicking with their left leg when their opponent has kicked with their right. It is hugely competitive and one of the most famous games in Ghana, so much so that there are people who want to make it an official sport.

Ampe is all about timing and you can easily be tricked, just as when a penalty is taken in a football match.

Every evening we would go outside, especially when the weather was beautiful, and I used to jump and jump and never get tired – childhood is something else!

My favourite childhood games were *Ampe* and *Mama na Papa*, when we cooked. It is a time in my life that is extremely special to me, and I am very grateful to God for being able to be a child and to take part in those events; it is an experience every child deserves. Playing outside for long periods of time did not feel dangerous at all, and we often played until midnight without our parents worrying that something would happen to us. We sometimes travelled for miles to visit friends who lived in neighbouring villages, but we always made it home. We were given complete freedom and there were rarely parents around to control us, which meant that if there was a misunderstanding, a fight might occur, leaving someone injured.

Childhood friends

My best friend when I was 12 years old was a girl called KorKor, or K.K. for short, and we did everything together. She was quite a quiet girl and very pretty, kind and respectful. For financial reasons, she was unable to continue her education around the time I left the village, but we had fantastic experiences together, sharing showers, playing football and swimming in the sea. Whenever I ran towards her and she saw me coming, I would make a noise a bit like a scream – I am a little bit jovial – and the people in her village would say, "What are you doing? Leave us alone!" We would then run off on our adventures.

K.K. spoke Adaa, which is different to my Ewe dialect, and I enjoyed learning from her and practising the words when I visited my neighbour Stephen and his wife, Mary, who also spoke K.K.'s language. They always appreciated my efforts and liked me as I would always try to make them smile.

K.K. and I cooked together and ate at her house, which was wonderful for me. Her upbringing was very different to my mine, in which my mum tried to remove me from poor uneducated people.

Another close, slightly older childhood friend was Celestina. Our mums have been best friends for years and she is like extended family. I have always kept in touch with her. She is also a Roman Catholic, and we met at the same Catholic Youth Organisation (CYO) and walked to church together. At this time, I did not know much about faith, but the church was a happy and exciting place, and we had fun during camping trips and sacraments. Every Sunday, we wore our uniforms, and when the Father entered the auditorium, we ushered him in while marching and playing the drums.

Chapter 6

Making Life Choices

Although I had never been taught dressmaking, my mum's skills were in my blood, and my siblings encouraged me to go into the profession because they said I was very creative. They also said there was plenty of money in it, advising me to ignore the government's secondary school set-up and to switch to fashion-design school instead. I was not happy at the time at Tema Secondary School. These were tough days for my mum too, as the 1981 coup had hit the fishing industry hard and had a negative impact on her business; however, she told me not to worry and that she would help me go to school, even if she had to sell her belongings. I harboured dreams of working as a secretary after I took a typing course at secondary school (I have a photograph of me at a typewriter) and was impressed by smartly dressed women working in offices, but my sisters were convinced that fashion school would be a better choice.

I chose to accept their advice. My dad said he would pay for a lady called Nicole to come to his big house to teach me, and in return, I would do chores. It was a similar arrangement to one that we had during my time at school and one that I think contributed to me failing my exams. I did not have much of a chance to study in between all the cooking, washing and childcare, and the balance of duties and studies was tricky. My dad's children were like my own children to me, and I took great care of them, keeping their hair lovely and nice. I miss them as they are all grown up now and they loved me so much, as did Janet. However, all this responsibility, combined with being away from my mum, meant I did not do well in my exams.

I knew I needed to move on with my life, so I chose to pursue a career in sewing under Nicole's tutorship, and she was so impressed that she said even people who finished the three-year course could not do what I was doing, yet it did not make me happy because it was not my passion. Nevertheless, I finished the course with a certificate and learnt a valuable lesson: sometimes your dreams cannot be truly realised and yet, it does not signify the end of the world; God always finds a way forward. It is written that, "all things work together for those who love the Lord" (Romans 8:28).

Putting food on the table

This belief was reinforced later in my life when I moved to the UK and wanted a work experience placement as part of an award I was completing in education and training. I came across a school called Broadway Academy in Birmingham, where, by chance, they were looking for an individual to provide short-term cover in a textile and food technician role. It fitted my skillset perfectly and they were very happy to have me. When I reflected on this, I thought, "Wow, this world is something else. You never know what tomorrow will bring to you. Yesterday, I refused the path my siblings were setting out for me, and now that very choice is putting food on my table." I now use this experience to offer people career advice. There was once a lady in my church who worked in business and was having difficulties finding a job. She was determined not to change her field of work, so I told her the value of having different skills and offered her the opportunity to work as a teaching assistant, with a view to the work leading somewhere. She now works for the council, but my experience helped her at the time.

I think it is important in life to take opportunities, to embrace even apparently small experiences that might be useful to our futures, and to listen to people's advice. On top of cooking and baking, I have also developed skills in juicing and blending, as well as completing a training course in nutrition and weight loss, all of which may provide something for me one day.

Inspirational influencers

Trouble will come, but I will deliver you out of it.

Psalm 50:15

I thank God that I am not where I used to be and feel very blessed that he favours me. I feel there is something unique about me that I have yet to discover.

I thank my siblings for putting in so much effort. I am especially grateful to my sister Olivia who bought my sewing machine for me, as well as my big brother, Frank, and my stepmum and dad, who were instrumental in my upbringing and throughout my education in Ghana.

Janet's sister Yaafio has also shown incredible generosity with both her time and advice, counselling me on potential career choices and treating me like a close member of her family. When I was 25 years old, she encouraged me to help her distribute medicines from the UK and America to pharmacies in Accra, educating me about which qualifications would help turn this skill into a viable profession. The course was too expensive for me; she, however, enrolled and is now a successful businesswoman in Ghana who owns two or three pharmacies and has built her own house.

I think my broad experience of living with adults as a young child really helped me get to where I am today in business. Living with someone who is not your biological parent encourages you to learn from them in way that you would not from your mum or dad. I learnt how to be submissive and how to cook, but also how to sell things. My aunty Vicky sold alcohol and cigarettes from her bar, Do Your Own Thing, and when I was a young teenager, I sometimes took these goods outside to sell in the streets before returning with her money. I carried a small bell, which I rang to catch people's attention, and I also sold and distributed to small shops. Similarly, when I lived with my mum and times were tough, we sold kerosene, charcoal, soap, bananas, oranges, eggs; anything that was trendy I carried around, and anything I came back with was something.

Helping my aunty and my mum taught me how to trade, to understand the value of things and to see what life looks like, and it really opened my eyes in a way not every young child experiences. Seeing life so explicitly makes you realise that if you do not make any effort, you do not gain anything.

Once, I was tempted to try alcohol so that I could understand how people got drunk. As I served a drink, I decided I wanted to try it, but I was scared, so I mixed it with water, which was the worst thing ever. The whole world started turning around and I could not do anything. I sat down and told my cousin what I had done. I was given something to help me vomit, which calmed me down, and then I ate some food and slept.

I started doing business from a very young age, and during my time at school, I always tried to sell something, such as toffee made from condensed milk, to allow me to buy small things for myself at the end of the day. I also went to the market to buy items such as pants, makeup and earrings, which I sold to people at school, offering them credit if they wanted to pay me back in instalments.

I realised I was growing into the role of a businesswoman early on and I sensed it was an experience that was quite unique to me, although my friend Celestina enjoyed it too. In the evening after school, she would set up a small stand outside her house, selling oranges, rice and stew, pancakes or *kelewele*, which is plantain mixed with spices and then fried. She used good ingredients, and her stall was popular with the smartly dressed passers-by who walked up and down the street on their nights out. People bought a lot from her; after all, everyone wants *kelewele* in the evening. Even now, it is traditional. As children,

Celestina and I inspired each other and had many conversations about what was selling well and what was not, and we are still very close. Celestina lives in Ghana with her husband, who is the headmaster of his father's school, where she used to work as a teacher, but she now runs a small restaurant, which she prefers.

Becoming a businesswoman

Once I had finished my sewing course, I jumped into starting a business buying and selling clothes and bags. My love of fashion took me to the city to purchase unique items for people to buy, and slowly, the business grew. Janet started working for the company, buying goods in the UK and transporting them to distributors in Ghana until, in 1999, we reached the point that we decided I should open my own boutique, Community One.

For three years, Janet rented the shop, which I managed on a day-to-day basis, until the owner decided to sell the premises and we successfully raised the money to buy it.

Community One sells outfits for famous people such as footballers' wives rather than ordinary people. It is not a big shop, but it has a good reputation. When I walked along the streets in Accra with my husband, Alfred, people would drive past and say, "Hey Angie, when did you arrive, did you bring goods?"

"You are too popular," Alfred would grumble.

Chapter 7

Family Affairs

My interest in business brought me closer to my stepmum, Janet. Our temperaments were well aligned, and we developed a good relationship, and while she had a strict nature, my humility and respect for her led her to love me. My siblings found our closeness difficult and would sometimes interpret it as favouritism, especially when we all lived together.

A brother's rage

My relationship with Janet became a problem for one of my brothers; he had been living in Accra but one day returned home to live with us with an intention I did not understand. He said our dad was growing old and we should do something to frustrate Janet into leaving him, otherwise she would take all his money. I advised him against doing this, highlighting how important it was for our dad to have a companion in his old age, and insisted we should leave them to enjoy their lives together. Once he saw that I supported Janet and would not cooperate with him, his approach changed and he became very negative towards me, refusing to talk further.

The tension between us reached a climax when, without asking, he took a food flask of mine that I kept in a special box, along with other treasured household items, in preparation for getting married one day. Upon his return from work, I discovered that the food he had stored in the flask had discoloured its pristine blue and white colours. I was upset and asked him why he had taken it, especially when he knew it was important to me. He stormed upstairs, angry.

At midnight that night when I – and everyone else in the house was fast asleep, he came into my room, still angry and very aggressive. "Take your food flask!" he shouted. "Take it and be careful in this house; if not, I will slap you." I woke with a start, wondering what had come over him, and asked why he was shouting and threatening to beat me. "If you talk again," he shouted, "I will slap you," and when I went to open my mouth, he made good his word. I screamed in pain and fear.

One of the occupants of the house that night was Janet's son Sammy, who was from a former relationship of hers. He did a lot of body building, winning the title of Mr Ghana. He emerged from his room, asking, "Why are you beating your little sister at this time of night?" My dad also appeared, but my brother told them to stay away and to stop interfering in business that was not their own. "Your sister is my sister too," Sammy told my brother, "and she is, moreover, a lady. You should not touch her." Sammy, who did not want a fight, stood with his hands held behind his back while my brother tried to provoke him. My dad then intervened and told everyone to go to bed.

The next morning, my dad told me that what had happened was not acceptable and that he needed to do something to resolve this situation. He contemplated calling the police to teach my brother a lesson, not knowing that he had woken early and already travelled to my sisters in Accra to tell them about the incident. A large group of my family returned in a van with my brother to attack me. I did not know what was going on, and in order to protect myself, I stayed in my room, closing my door and the curtains. They came into the house, ran up the stairs and began banging on my door, accusing me of being an evil child and conniving with our stepmum against my brother.

I knelt on my bedroom floor, recalling a scripture in the Bible from Second Chronicles, 20:22, in which God speaks to Jehoshaphat as his enemies approach. "You do not need to fight this battle," God said. "Just stand and gather yourself in worship and praise." Jehoshaphat listens and guides his followers in praise and worship to God. Similarly, I did not feel I could fight this battle alone, but with God's strength, I found myself able to stand.

"God, the battle belongs to you," I said, and I began singing in worship, while my siblings continued banging on the door and shouting at me. Feeling that it was not safe for me to open the door, I remained on my knees, praying and hoping God would intervene. I could hear my dad outside, explaining his version of events, and although my siblings refused to believe him, the mood soon calmed and they and my brother left the house.

Sammy travelled to Accra to talk to my brother, but several days later, he had still not returned. News then reached us that he had been in a very serious motorbiking accident and was in a grave condition in hospital. At work in Janet's shop when I heard the news, I closed up immediately and left for the hospital. There I saw his whole body in a terrible state, his ear scraped away. I prayed, telling God to step in because I know there is nothing too challenging for him; after all, he even raised the dead back to life. "Please," I begged, "I want Sammy to live, I don't want Janet to hear this story." All sorts of thoughts went through my head. I wondered if all this was because of me.

I contacted Pastor Hagan and Pastor Frimpong to support my prayers, and when I returned to the hospital, the doctor said a miracle had occurred. The medical team had placed Sammy in a condemned ward, fearing he was about to die, when suddenly his fortunes changed and there was now hope of a recovery. The doctor said they were not sure how much his recovery was down to his physical strength, for although he had been effectively dead, yet his resilient heart continued to pump. I cried so much that the doctors wondered if I was his wife.

Sammy was taken out of intensive care and relocated to the main ward, for which our family and the wider community were so grateful. I continued to pray and say my Beautiful Amen, with a joyful smile and the belief that all would be well: God had finished the battle and it had been won. We called Janet with the news, and she was so relieved as he had been involved in quite a few close shaves during his life. Now with only one ear, he still bears the very visible scars of this accident.

God is amazing, and while we do not see him face to face, he appears to us in various ways. I felt his presence when I was on my knees in my room, and I saw him doing his work after Sammy's accident. If it was not God, then who else? God is always there for us, and I want to encourage people to call on him; pick up the phone and dial Jeremiah 33:3, and he will answer your prayers.

The fallout

My siblings continued to attack me over concerns that our inheritance would bypass us and benefit Janet, as the widow, and their shared son Richard. I continued to disagree with them and remember overhearing Janet teasing my dad about his many children and what a headache it would be to share his properties among them all.

She did not expect any inheritance and always helped out with his business, even selling some of her properties to support him. I kept reminding my siblings that thinking negatively would lead to something evil because what they thought may not be true, and even if our worst fears were realised, even if Janet claimed something, that would be OK; after all, she was with him for years.

I respect Janet; she is a very nice, straightforward, generous person who cares deeply for people, and I always treated her like another mother. She has a kind heart and had accepted all my dad's children, never expecting Richard to have everything. Instead, she supported and helped me and my siblings. I was very quiet following all the rows, and when Janet saw this, she tried to shake me out of my trance, urging me to ignore my siblings' words and move on with my life. She drew parallels with Joseph and his envious siblings in the Bible, reminding me that God lifted Joseph and blessed him. I have never forgotten those words and appreciate how important it is to have someone to be there to lift you when life is hard.

My dad instigated a family meeting, which he hoped would help settle the issue, but it became more complicated once Janet realized his properties were at the heart of the struggle and the reason that my siblings wanted to fight Sammy. My dad had accumulated a vast wealth, which included properties such as a mansion in Community 10 and another in Accra, and swathes of land, as well as shares. Janet cut our discussions short, peacefully explaining that, "In this life, I came with nothing. I came naked and naked I'll go, even if I'm buried with clothes,

I'm still naked. All these possessions are worldly things. Take your property; I'm going."

"Come back, come back," the family said, and my dad called her, but she left. The meeting was over.

No turning back

Three days later, I returned home to find Janet packing her belongings. "Sister, what's happening?" I asked.

"This hatred for me is too much," she replied, sombrely. "I need to go." I begged her to stay and care for my dad, but he had not done enough to protect her. She insisted that she was leaving and would go to live with her sister in Community 11. I had to break the news to my poor dad when he returned home and he was so dejected and upset, begging me to phone her for him.

"Papa, Richard and I did our best," I told him, "but she refused our pleas." I was able to get hold of her on the phone, but once she heard my father's voice, she hung up.

The fallout from the event was enormous; my dad began questioning what I had done to make my siblings hate me so much, and Janet's overwhelming sense of shame led her to leave Ghana. She felt her life had been wasted and that her friends would laugh at her. She had no place to sleep, despite our offers, and insisted on fighting for a property of her own, for herself. I became an intermediary, with my dad calling me to explain how much he loved her, and I suggesting he provide some land to build a self-contained house for her to live alone. Janet laughed at this: "See," she said. "He has money, but I do not want anything!"

She gathered her documents, went to the US embassy for an interview and soon received a five-year travel visa. She organised herself very fast, asking me not to tell my dad where she was going. Before long, she was on a flight, and it was not until she reached America that she agreed to talk to him. He was devastated, and from that day forwards, he was an unhappy man.

Miraculously, Janet found a job within three days of her arrival in the US, and within three months, she began sending money back to the family, enabling them to build two beautiful houses on her land. She also entrusted her entire boutique shop to me, saying that I deserved it and asking me to take good care of it. "If you make it good, you'll enjoy it," she told me. "If you destroy it, it's up to you."

I was completely overwhelmed as I had assumed the shop would pass to her younger sister or to Richard, but she said that her gift was the result of my humility and that I should continue to be a good child. I was very happy when she handed me the key, although it did confirm my siblings' unfounded thoughts that I had engineered such an outcome. I was not her blood daughter, but my humility brought me far. There is a saying that a person with real humility knows how much they are loved.

If you humble yourself, He will lift you.

Janet has returned to Ghana to live, and we chat regularly.

CHAPTER 8

Growing Up

My siblings' visits to our dad waned and, in the end, I was left to care for him. Tensions continued, to the point that one of my sisters became irritated when I moved belongings around the house or walked around singing. One particular day, I woke early before church, and as I ironed my clothes I sang, "I have joy in my heart, deep deep down in my heart. Jesus gave it to me and no one can destroy." She stood next to me and began shouting, asking who I thought wanted to destroy me. I did not understand and, speaking honestly, the hostility became so bad that I nearly pushed myself into a relationship that I was not ready for just so that I could leave the house. It had all become too much for me.

Unwanted attention

At 25 years old, I had been a bridesmaid to my siblings and witnessed the beauty of marriage, all the while dreaming that my dad would one day give me away to my future husband. I used to pray a Beautiful Amen when I thought about this, but I knew I needed to be married before I left our family house. An older man, a Ghanaian from Germany and from a different church to mine, drove past me one day and offered me a lift home, after which he became intent on pursuing me. He was very persistent, offering to buy me a new house, showing me where it would be, sending sofas for this proposed dwelling to my family home. Divorced and with grown-up children, he was 45 years old, and this age difference felt too big – he was just too old. I was brought up to respect those older than me, and while I was able to say no to him, it was difficult to be honest about the reasons behind my decision. It is different in the UK, where children are free to ask questions and to be involved in adult conversation; in Ghana a more reverential attitude exists between the younger and older generations.

My suitor once came to the house to tell my dad he would take great care of me, attempting to prove his worth by showing Alfred the keys to a car that he wanted to give me. When he left, I was able to tell my dad it did not feel right and that I wanted to wait for the right person. My reservations were confirmed by a local pastor, who had prayed for me after I gave him and his family some vegetables. He told me he was good friends with the man and knew of his intention to marry me, but he felt that the man's temperament was not right and warned me, "My dear daughter, be careful not to enter into such a relationship." My fears confirmed, I shed tears of joy; once again I sensed the presence of God telling me to go the right way, not the wrong way.

The following day, the man returned to our house and, as was his custom, parked his car outside, beeping the horn while he waited. This time, I refused to go out, but he begged me to, so I decided to give him my final word.

"Today is the last time you come to this compound," I told him, "and if you come again, I'll call the police."

He retaliated angrily to my rejection: "Do you think you are beautiful? There are many women, not just you." Swerving his car sharply as if in a final parting shot, he drove away. I watched the back of his car dwindle into the distance, thanking God for my life; I never set eyes on him again.

When I was nearly 28 years old, I received a marriage proposal from my lovely friend Opoku, who was very handsome and popular with women. However, as soon as his parents discovered that I was Ewe, not Ashanti, they were angry, for the Ewe and Ashanti tribes have been divided for centuries, although attitudes are starting to soften with the help of Christianity, which encourages people to see God as a leader of all nations and all colours.

"You will never bring a lady from the Ewe tribe into this house," Opoku's parents told him.

I found Opoku's description of his family's rejection of me alarming, and I decided that, even though he was young, handsome and well-todo, marrying him would be a mistake. I always had a strong vision of my future and prayed I would find a relationship which included the love and support of all the immediate family.

My bold reaction angered Opoku and he kept pursuing me, even phoning with the lure of an American visa he had secured and promising to wait until I was ready to commit. I did not listen and eventually deleted his number from my phone. The experience taught me the importance of choosing your own path and doing what makes you happy.

I did not tell my mum, Regina, about these personal struggles because I found it difficult and did not want to burden her with my troubles, and I fought on alone. Christianity has saved me from feeling totally isolated though; it offers a sweet and beautiful battle which, if you are able to withstand it, rewards with a victorious crown. The ultimate prize is found in heaven, but I have been lucky enough to experience crowns such as Janet bestowing her shop on me, which was an honour. I am grateful I found God at an early age, otherwise I may not have been able to withstand these challenges.

Biding my time

One day in 2001, a local pastor who Janet had previously noticed was interested in me called in at my shop to discuss church affairs. Soon after he left, Janet phoned from America, and I told her he had visited. "Can't you see he's in love with you?" she asked me. I got to know the pastor quite well in my role as a Sunday school teacher, but I knew, deep down, that I did not want to marry a pastor owing to the pressures and stresses associated with his job, and I was conscious that I should not make the wrong choice.

Before long, a message was sent to our church (now called Royalhouse Chapel International) from the headquarters' Apostle General, Sam Korankye Ankrah, and his wife, explaining that they wanted to ordain this same pastor but could not do so until he was married. They were looking for the best person for him and suggested I should think about it.

I quickly told the apostle's wife, Mama Rita, a beautiful woman with a beautiful spirit, "Mummy, you know what, I have somebody abroad I am waiting for." This was not true for I did not, in fact, have anybody! Such details did not matter to Mama Rita anyway.

"Ignore them," she told me in her characteristically commanding way. "Those people abroad will let you down." Nevertheless, I stood firm and refused the marriage arrangement, hoping for a more suitable match.

I did not have to wait long until a good friend of mine called Mrs Pyne – who Janet introduced me to at church – told me about JoJo, a nurse at Korle-Bu hospital. Mrs Pyne has a beautiful heart; her involvement in my life is a blessing, and while I was still single, she and her husband, an Indian man living in Ghana, always included me in their social life. They would book me into hotels in Winneba and the Cape Coast, as well as inviting me to important gatherings with parliamentary members. I already knew JoJo was a good man and a Christian, but Mrs Pyne persuaded me to become better acquainted with him. What I did not know, however, was that he was on the cusp of travelling to the UK in two weeks' time, having already secured his visas. It felt very quick, a bit of a whirlwind. He took me out, promised me much, introduced me to his parents, met my dad and vowed to organise our marriage permit when he got to the UK. He would, he said, then fetch me as soon as possible.

I decided to go for it, feeling incredibly grateful and thanking God for the opportunity. Once he had left for the UK, however, his phone calls became intermittent, and then I did not hear from him for a long time. I wondered what was going on and confided in a friend, who told me not to worry, so I continued to endure the wait. After a few months, JoJo called me at my shop to say, "Angie, please, I want us to talk." He said something was bothering him and because he loved me, he wanted to share it so that I could have a good future. He assured me he had not met anyone else but that UK life was totally different to what he had anticipated; processes were slower than he had expected and he did not want to waste my time. He urged me not to wait for him, to think about my future and health, and to accept a man if he came my way. He promised to take good care of

69

himself and focus completely on God. We finished talking, and despite the intense disappointment and pain, I returned home thinking that he was a wonderful man with unique compassion: he was one in a million.

My experience with JoJo made me realise that God had plans for me and knew what lay ahead. Even though the devil had started to fight, I had survived and so I cast my mind back to count all the blessings in my life. I decided to close the chapter on JoJo, and his relief at my decision was palpable. He began calling more and we became close friends.

Chapter 9

Finding Love and My Own Family

Wary of men after my experience with JoJo, I decided to focus my efforts on the church. I attended a programme called Children's Day at Royalhouse Chapel, Tema, with a lady called Gladys, at which our photograph was taken. This photograph was to change the course of my life.

There is a saying that even if you have your life mapped out, things happen that shape your destiny in a way you might never imagine. At the time, Alfred Nartey Accam, my future husband, lived in Spain, and while visiting a friend out there, he saw the photograph and recognized me. He had, it transpired, seen me previously outside his tailoring shop in Tema market, Community 1. After learning that I was single, Alfred, who had been praying to meet his future wife, asked his friend for my number and decided to give it a try.

His phone call to the shop was completely out of the blue; he was very upbeat and jovial, saying, "I know you; do you know me?"

"No, I do not," I replied, putting down the phone.

Alfred persisted, describing himself to me and mentioning places that were familiar, but I felt I was being pranked, so I put the phone down again. He then called back and said, "Get ready, I'm coming to marry you!" Alfred was keen to speed up our courtship, while I kept encouraging him to calm down.

By now, Mrs Pyne and I were more than sisters; she had watched me repeatedly refuse the advances of pastors who kept coming my way, and she was one of the people who kept encouraging me onwards, reminding me not to miss an opportunity. She was my best friend and certainly instrumental in my union with Alfred. She told me to tread carefully, to consider Alfred as a potential suitor and to listen to Aunty Rose, who had come to the shop and described him as a good Christian.

The next time he called, I engaged in conversation with him, and he behaved himself, talking like a man who was seriously in need of something. He told me he used to watch my sister Olivia and me packing the goods she imported from Nigeria and how, as a tailor who made dresses and suits, he often used our materials. Olivia distributed items such as buttons and linings to many businesses and Alfred's shop would sew garments for us to then sell on. While we were not friends at this point, we knew each other by sight and would say hello before he went abroad and went missing from the system.

Alfred's love of travelling began in his early 20s, when he was motivated to find greener pastures. Before he settled in Spain, he visited Liberia, Cote d'Ivoire, Turkey, Russia, Greece and Guinea-Bissau, at one point working in the engine rooms of fishing trawlers.

A church champion

Despite these comforting connections, I remained determined to find someone in Ghana. When I was about 28 years old, I attended an event in Accra organised by our church Apostle General, Sam Korankye Ankrah, and his wife, Mama Rita. It was a packed programme in the University of Legon involving every branch of the Royal Ladies Camp Meeting, and I was asked to sing and lead the worship. I was very scared and on edge with nerves, developing a fever and a cough the day before for which I attempted home remedies, but nothing worked. I boldly visited Mama Rita to ask her to explain to her husband that I was not well enough to perform; however, she said, "Whether you like it or not, God wants you to do it."

She was very good at motivating us and I saw there was no escape, instead choosing to pray. We camped for three days, praying and fasting, until the time came ... and it was miraculous. I do not know what I actually did, but afterwards, everybody was shaking me, and the instrumentalists came over to say, "Well done, that was so powerful."

Mrs Pyne said to me, "Angie, look at my body. You overwhelmed me. I'm freezing. The Holy Spirit came upon you; it was unique and I've never seen anything like it." Mrs Pyne and I went back to our dormitory and were followed by two ladies who called our names and asked to touch me so I could anoint them with the power of God.

Mama Rita was the mother of the church, a first lady; she oversaw the women's and children's departments and gave me my job as a Sunday school teacher. I took this role very seriously and found that working with children was amazing; I loved teaching them about Jesus Christ and how to fear and love God. I completed training courses with a girl called Rose Darling in which we learnt how to guide the children, choreographing plays and helping them memorise the Bible and poems. I later became president of the Sunday school department, and I have videos of the performances we organised. I miss those children, who are now big boys and girls; some are even married.

Indirectly, it was the church that brought me back to Alfred. One day while I was dancing during an offering at church, the apostle called me over. "I just saw a vision of you standing between two men and you were confused, not knowing who to choose," he told me, "but I want to tell you that the one who is after you is the one for you." He told me to pray for it to happen.

"I told you!" my friend said. "God has revealed it to the apostle; just accept it."

Persistence pays

I began responding to Alfred's calls and within two months, although he was based in Spain, he began forcing me to visit his parents. It felt too quick, but he assured me that I had been with him for many years in spirit and that God had revealed I was the best woman for him, so I needed to get ready. He was very persistent and impatient, calling to describe exactly where his mum's house was located. I wondered if this was the doing of the Lord – it was intense. I finally went to visit his parents, who were called Mr Williams and Rita, and his mum immediately embraced me, introducing me to her friends and referring to me as her in-law. I was very happy, experiencing the feeling of a perfect inner peace.

My mother-in-law, who we call by her nickname, Maalee, has been like a mother to me. God sent this wonderful woman into my life, and we share such a strong mutual love for one another. People complain bitterly about their mothers-in-law or stepmums, but my experience is positive; both Janet and

74

Maalee are beautiful inside and out. If I ever have a small disagreement with my husband, Maalee will always be understanding and comfort me, and she never bothered us when we lived in Spain. We would call her to organise sending something to her in Ghana, but she would encourage us to satisfy ourselves before thinking about her. My father-in-law was also wonderful and very jovial. After our wedding, once my husband had returned to Spain, he would regularly check in with me, and the first thing he would say was, "Hi baby! How are you?" He used to love my salads, so I would always make sure I had some ready for him when he visited. He passed away in 2015.

Alfred was keen to speak to my pastor so that we could begin counselling together, and I also spoke to my pastor, who said he could see Alfred's commitment to God, and a seriousness in him which was not common for a man of his age. He felt Alfred was the right choice, especially after speaking to his pastor in Spain, who provided context and the reassurance that Alfred was hard-working and a good match.

Between June and December 2001, my husband began sending money back to Ghana so that I could buy items to prepare for our marriage – cloth, handbags, dresses for me, drinks, traditional clothes for my dad, mum, siblings and brothers-in-law. There was so much to prepare, and while the money would usually go directly to the mother of an African family, he wanted me to have the money to allow me to choose what I liked. By December, we were ready to fix a wedding date, something the pastor said was unusual and against the constitution, but he agreed to break the protocol for us. Usually, we would have had six months of continuous counselling together ahead of our marriage, but in those days, there was no Zoom, so we did our counselling in our respective countries before uniting for a three-day intensive counselling session when Alfred arrived in Ghana.

My husband and my dad got on well from the beginning and I was so excited to see them together. My dad's priority was to ensure I was happy, and once he knew we were committed and loved one another, he was content. He would not judge someone on their colour, job or background, rather, he wanted to be sure the union would be a peaceful one. The two of them got on well, cracking jokes and talking at length on the telephone.

While my dad did not talk much, when he wanted to joke, he would. The first thing he told my future husband, Alfred, after being asked for my hand in marriage, was, "Don't forget to bring my Coca-Cola." Our dad's love of the drink was a family joke and when a suitor visited, his first consideration would always be, "Two crates of Coca-Cola please." His approach was different to many fathers in Ghana, who expected to be given a dowry in the form of a cow or other high value items, a demanding approach that would often scare men off. Other Ghanaian traditions include a process known as *Acontasika*, in which payments are made to prospective brothers-in-law, as well as gifting expensive drinks to the woman's family.

However, my dad adopted a simpler method, a list of four criteria, which he asked in order of importance:

"Are you a Christian?"

"What job do you have?"

"Where are you from?"

"Do you love her?"

This list was always closely followed by, "… and don't forget two crates of Coca-Cola."

His endearing relationship with this sugary drink featured prominently in his friendship with my husband, who would always buy him Coca-Cola before returning to Spain. Whenever they spoke on the phone, the last words you would hear would always be, "… and don't forget two crates of Coca-Cola."

Destined to marry a pastor

Right up until I met Alfred, I had actively tried to avoid marrying a pastor, eager to be free from the stresses I envisaged were associated with that line of work. When Alfred came my way, I believed he was not a pastor and so I accepted him, but, fast-forward a number of years, he was ordained as a deacon and I became a pastor's wife after all. We must learn to follow God's purpose and not lean on our own understanding as whatever is written, is written, and we cannot change it.

I draw parallels with the story of Jonah. God asks him to preach in the city of Nineveh, but fear makes Jonah run away and take a ship to a different town. During his journey, God takes action and the sea becomes rough, nearly sinking the boat. Those aboard begin to panic; the sea had been calm and their progress peaceful up until now. Jonah explains that he is the cause of this sudden change and asks to be thrown into the sea to restore order. He is then swallowed by a whale, which swims to the shore of the exact place God intended Jonah to visit.

Being a pastor's wife is sweet and beautiful, but the challenges that accompany it can be painful. Wherever you go, people respect, adore, love, hail and pamper you, but the more people there who hail you, the more chance there is that others hate you. I do sometimes wish I was an ordinary church member who could go to church, say my prayers and return peacefully. No one will complain about the little mistakes a church member makes, but the smallest mistake by a pastor's wife will be interpreted very differently. God calls you into the role, so you have to endure the pain; it is the metaphorical cross you carry. It is not easy, so I thank God for giving me the strength to do it all. I have only Mondays free, and I am responsible for the women in the church, the Sunday school department and prayers. On Tuesdays, I hold a women's prayer meeting and on Wednesdays, I have a church Zoom meeting. On Thursdays, I pray collectively for the nation, for Ghana and for the whole world with a group of people called Sisters of Hope from different churches. On Fridays I go to church with my family, and every first Saturday of the month I meet with a marriage group that I have set up.

Our wedding

Alfred and I married on 5th January 2002; it was a beautiful moment and I felt I had the whole world. Everything was ready when Alfred arrived in Ghana – the invitations printed and sent, food ordered, tables organised, all the important details catered for – to allow him to concentrate on family and friends. Prior to my marriage, I was on a broken bridge, waiting to fall down, but God paved a way for me. Everything came together very quickly during that period, and I was so happy that God had provided for me. My dream had been to find a man to marry so I could move away from my dad's home, and after enduring a painful wait, I saw God's hands at work.

The wedding was well organised by myself and Mrs Pyne, and my stepmum's younger sister Yaafio took me to Accra to choose quality clothes before we returned to prepare for the big day. My family played a major role in the event, especially on my mother's side; they were all very happy for me. A few from my father's side could not attend owing to our family problems, and neither could Janet, who was in the USA, or 12 of my 14 siblings, but this did not bother me. I took comfort in the Bible's message: "Those who are with us are more than those who are against us." I realised that even though they could not make it, God would still bring people to give me joy.

I find it hard to understand the depths of some people's love, especially that of my stepparents, who are fantastic and have set an example to the world. People hear the word stepmum and make negative assumptions, but I am always proud to talk about Janet. At the time of our wedding, she was in America and unable to attend, but she told her friends in the UK that her daughter was getting married and asked them to represent her. Yaa, one of Janet's sisters, was in the UK when she heard and insisted on flying to Ghana with her husband and daughter to be part of our celebrations. When I saw them at our wedding, I was overwhelmed, thinking, "Wow, am I this special?" The next day, my dad asked how I knew all these people and I said, "I don't know; it's the favour of God."

He was shocked. "If I had known," he said, "I would have called the press to take photographs to put in the newspaper." Among all his daughters' weddings, this was the biggest, a real super-wedding.

Right Reverend Jonny, who came to represent the Apostle General, saw how happy my husband was when we were in the church, exclaiming, "Why, you're in such a rush! I've blessed many marriages, but I've never seen anyone this desperate to get married." If you watch the video, you can see how happy everyone is, clapping and dancing, the glory of God expressed through an atmosphere of joy. I made 250 wedding invitations and planned to stick to that number, but we calculated enough food and drink for 350 people, and it all went. We felt very special that all these people came because of us.

We also received an incredibly generous gift from a very rich and popular woman in Ghana, known as Top Lady, for whom I sourced unique and special outfits for events through my boutique. When she heard about our wedding, she offered us her hotel for the reception and said she would provide everything free of charge. My husband was in awe of this gesture.

My dad was happy for us, but the reality of my move to Spain soon began to dawn on him. He called me to say he wanted to speak to my husband to see if, after the marriage and our honeymoon, I could stay with him. My husband planned to rent a house for me in Ghana until my documents were ready for me to travel to Spain, but my dad said this was a waste of money and offered up a room in his house. I realised my dad needed someone with him – I felt it and so did my husband. Having sensed my dad's loneliness, my husband was keen not to upset him, so he agreed and felt at peace, knowing I was safe and living under my dad's roof.

PART TWO

LIFE IN GHANA AFTER MARRIAGE

Chapter 10

A Test Before a Testimony

I lived with my dad until I became pregnant with twins, a boy and a girl. The plan was for me to give birth in Spain, but the process of applying for a visa was long and complicated and would have involved me sleeping at the Spanish embassy in order to join the long queues. Even then, a meeting was not guaranteed and sometimes embassy staff would see only five people in one day, which would require me to make a return trip. We decided it was not a good idea during my pregnancy, so I waited.

My beautiful twins

I began having contractions a few days before the seventh month of my pregnancy and gave birth to my babies. I called them Emmanuel and Emmanuella, names that mean, "God is with us." Emmanuel looked very dark, like his dad, while Emmanuella was very fair and beautiful. I do not know what happened after their birth, but all of a sudden, the medics said that the oxygen being given to the babies had turned off, so they had to rush them to a different clinic. It was late and the doctor was not around, and by the time he arrived, Emmanuel had gone. The girl remained very active and so they referred us to the main hospital, where the standard of care was very poor. I lost both babies within four days. It was a very sad and difficult time and had a detrimental effect on me.

It happened on my birthday.

I delivered the twins on my birthday: 10th July 2002. My husband called to wish me happy birthday, but I was broken, downcast, in pieces. The twins were our bundles of joy, and he was shocked by the unexpected news; we shed tears. It was not easy for him to cope, but because he is a man, he needed to be strong and let life go on.

I had been so happy to be expecting twins, it was beautiful news. My mum had twins, Franklin also had twins, it was a miracle, and then, so suddenly, they disappeared.

I said to God, "WHY?"

"I am a Sunday school teacher, I love children, why me?"

I wept on my knees and said a Beautiful Amen. I accepted it and understood that the sacred things belong to Him alone. I was encouraged by the kind words of a pastor who told me that when he was praying for me, God revealed to him that I could have died in childbirth but that he saved my life, saved his Queen, to restore me. The pastor urged me to stop crying, assuring me that there would be a restoration and I should pull myself together.

The stigma made going out difficult for me, and I did not leave the house for days. Even before the twins' births, people speculated that I was pregnant before I got married, despite being a Christian. Alfred had been in Ghana for only 21 days and because they were twins, my stomach showed early. I was mad and heartbroken and did not go out to the shops, choosing to stay indoors and cry, closing my door so I did not have to talk to anybody, or eat. Fear overwhelmed me, but Richard, my dad and Janet tried to encourage me, saying I should endure it and that God would provide again.

"You'll have children; more than your expectation," my dad said to me. "It's unfortunate your husband is not here with you, otherwise you would get pregnant again."

I am so grateful that when challenges have come my way, God has sent people from my family and from the church, to lift and strengthen me. Pastor Veronica visited to share her experiences of pain, inspiring me with anecdotes of how she endured the loss of her husband. If you do not have people around you, you can be left demoralised and weak, but I was lucky to have a wonderful support network.

A mother of many nations

The loss of children is indescribable for a mother; I saw my twins and then, all of a sudden, they were ruptured out of my hands. The pain I felt was compounded by my sister Olivia's twins, as well as the twins of my brother Richard. On my dad's side, out of the siblings, there were five of us who had twins. One day I prayed, crying and crying, until I heard a voice which said, "Why are you doing this to yourself. Have you no God? Pull yourself together." The sound seemed far away, but it was enough to make me open my eyes. I went straight to the shower to refresh myself, returned to my room, got dressed, took one of my prettiest handbags and decided to go out. I went outside with my chest up, appearing happy to observers, and when I got to the market, people commiserated, but they were surprised by the way I dressed and behaved. I decided life must go on and I began putting myself back together. I went out freely, sharing the scripture, "Pleasant are they who go through persecution and challenges, for they shall be rewarded" (Matthew 5:10–12).

Serving God is so sweet, but there are many obstacles in life and when these experiences come, you must stand firm. The Bible likens it to Jesus's suffering on the cross and how, just as He was victorious, we too will emerge victorious from our troubles. I now understand that before you can give a testimony, you must first go through a test. The birth and subsequent death of my twins was my test, and this is my testimony. I now have a message which I can touch somebody's heart with, somebody who is perhaps in more pain than I was, somebody I can help. One of our brothers from the church described me as 'a mother of many nations', referring to the many different people I would talk to after my personal test. He said God has bestowed me with this title so that I could help fix the broken-hearted and put a smile back on their faces.

I leave the battle to you

Thanks be to God, owing to the support of those around me, I was able to retain my faith. Some may go through situations like this and decide not to worship Him any more, but I still love God and even though it is painful, I choose to endure it and take joy from knowing I am a partaking in His suffering. The Bible says that even though we go through trauma and persecutions, we should remember we are sharing the suffering Jesus went through on the cross.

It was not an easy time at all; I was very isolated and cried often, but I used worship to encourage myself over the years. The Bible says, "You need not fight this battle, you just stand firm and see the salvation of the Lord" (Second Chronicles 20:17), and this verse empowered me enough to say, "OK, God, I leave the battle to you."

I also took comfort in the story of Job, a wealthy man who the Devil tempts to see if his piety is real, or merely rooted in his prosperity. God tells the Devil, "You can do what you want to Job, but his heart belongs to me." The Devil then kills Job's children, but instead of blaming God, Job falls to his knees and says, "You gave them to me, so if you have taken them back, glory be to you." Desperate for Job to deny God, the Devil burns nearly his whole body, but still he refuses to leave God. "God," the Devil says, "look, he still loves you."

This story always gives me hope that one day there will be restoration for me in the same way that God brought everything back to Job – his children, his cattle and his money. Even in the depths of my pain, I received those words and trusted in God.

Visions of a visa

It was very hard for my husband to hear the news of the twins over the phone, and he was desperate for me to be with him in Spain. He managed to track down the Ghanaian ambassador's personal telephone number to ask why my visa had been refused. The ambassador wanted to know how he had found the number, but my husband said, "That's not the issue now. Please issue the visa for Angelina or I'll keep calling you."

The ambassador was eager to meet my husband, who spoke fluent Spanish, and invited us to the embassy for an interview in October 2002. He kept asking how my husband had got his number. "You know what," my husband replied, "when you give Angelina her visa, I'll tell you!" Prompted by recent events that had intensified his desire to have me alongside him in Spain,

Alfred then took dramatic steps. When the ambassador asked us to wait so he could attend an emergency meeting, my husband stood in front of his car, saying, "I need my wife and I'm not letting you go; let's go inside and talk." The ambassador promised to do his best and said I would have my visa within the next six weeks.

After leaving the embassy, we hailed a taxi before deciding to stop briefly so Alfred could buy some plantain, something he had not eaten for a while. It was not until we were home and opening the front door that we realised he had, distracted by the food, left all our important visa documents in the back of the taxi. He handed me the plantain and shot out of the door, running at full speed to trace the taxi, which held the keys to our future life: our marriage certificate, my passport and our visa interview.

We spent hours looking for the taxi and reported the incident to the police, as well as paying local radio stations up to 200,000 Ghanaian Cedi to make an announcement. The recovery of the file was critical as we had only six weeks to claim our visa, and I did not have time to apply for a new passport. One, two, three and four weeks passed, but still we had no news. Every day I cried and prayed, not understanding why all these terrible things were happening to me.

I decided to visit Mama Rita after something told me I should sew a seed in the life of her young son, Paapa, by giving him an offering with a purpose. Such acts mirror the Bible's story of feeding the 5,000 (John 6:1–14), when Jesus takes five small loaves of bread and two small fish and successfully provides food for everyone, and more. It teaches us that if you have faith in the little seed you are planting, it can germinate into whatever you are looking for in abundance. I put some money in an envelope and went to the church where I told Mama Rita about my problem, asking to be remembered in her prayers. She said, "Angie, don't worry, you'll go to your husband whether the Devil likes it or not."

Soon, with only six days left, I went to church and decided to cry like a baby. I thought about how a child calls for the attention of its parents and I chose to cry and disturb God until he attended to me. The pastor's opening words were, "Finally, Devil, you cannot trouble me because I wear on my forehead the mark of Jesus Christ" (Galatians 6:17). Once I heard this verse, I knew my problems were coming to an end and this would be my final day of suffering before salvation.

On my way home, the Holy Spirit told me to tell my younger brother what I was going through in case he knew someone who could quickly process a passport for me. He was the only person I had talked to about my problem and later that day, as I escorted my friend Esther to the bus stop, I heard him shouting loudly for me. I ran back to the house where he told me excitedly that somebody had just called my phone to say they had the documents. It was incredible to think that if I had not shared my story with him, he would have been unaware of the situation and possibly told the people on the phone that they had the wrong number.

I was over the moon, but also scared as I had no proof that the call was legitimate, and I did not want to be robbed or kidnapped. My brother and one of Alfred's sisters kindly offered to go with me. We had agreed to meet the people with my documents at a specific time, but we hit a huge traffic jam and were trapped for so long that I was ready to jump out of the van and walk. By the time we got to the meeting place, the people had left.

We stood in disbelief until a boy from the communications centre where the people with my documents had made the call told us about a woman who had accompanied them and might know something. We traced her to the church, and as soon as she saw me, she said, "Wow. Woman – are you the one? God loves you so much, but do you know what, the Devil is a liar and they want to destroy your future, but they will not." She said she had tried everything to persuade the men to leave the file, but they had taken it away.

The woman, a seller of *koko*, which is a bit like porridge, had been approached on the street by the brother of the taxi driver, who showed her the documents and said, "I've seen this in my brother's car for some time now and I don't know why he is keeping it and why he has not reported it." The brother told her how his heart would beat every time he saw the documents, and once the woman saw my passport picture, tears rolled down her cheeks. They were keen to find a telephone number in order to reunite it with its owner.

God visits us in unique ways and I saw him working on my behalf through the taxi driver's brother, as well as via the miracle *koko* seller. She told me, "You are blessed, and no one can stop your destiny. Come back tomorrow morning for your documents." The Bible says, "Whoever is kind to the poor, lends to the Lord, and he will reward them for what they have done" (Proverbs 19:17). I returned with George, my husband's elder brother, and Wofa, the taxi driver, was there, as she had anticipated, with an intact file. I thought, "Thank you, Jesus. Thank you, God. Finally the battle is won." However, the taxi driver said we must pay him before he would return the file. George was furious, but I reminded him that there are some battles you must fight wisely and that we needed to allow God to do his work. We were nearly there, but we needed to cross the Red Sea peacefully and without violence.

I asked the man if he was a Christian, which he said he was. I said it was a shame, for a true Christian would not ask for money and would have taken the file to a police station in order to reunite it with its owner. "Do not withhold good from someone who deserves it, when it is in your power to do so" (Proverbs 3:27). I also asked him where the *koko* seller was, and he said she was not there and had travelled. I said, "God, is she an angel? She's disappeared." I never set eyes on her again and I do not know who she was, but I know God used her to break down barriers, ensuring I got my visa four days later.

During this process, I learned to trust people, for my brother was instrumental in reuniting me with the documents. I also learnt not to give up; when a miracle is knocking at your door, you must go the extra mile, and open the door to your success.

The Devil is always close by

The turmoil of 2002, which had begun when I lost my babies and was exacerbated by the drama surrounding my Spanish visa, grew progressively worse when I nearly lost my closest friendship. I felt that everything in my life was in disarray.

This impossibly hard period taught me many important lessons, one of which was that some friends can be very dangerous and you cannot trust everybody in the church. Sadly, it was my great friendship with Mrs Pyne that fell victim to the reality that whenever there is love and unity, the Devil is always close by, waiting to separate and destroy it. I compare this to the story of Adam and Eve in the Garden of Eden, where God created a perfect world, entrusting everything to them until the Devil came to deceive the couple and create confusion. In the case of Mrs Pyne and me, the Devil used somebody else to come between us, but thankfully, we realised and were able to reconcile.

Before I lost our twins, I attended a church programme in which we fasted and prayed in groups which corresponded to the month we were born. I joined the relatively small 'July' group while heavily pregnant and prayed intensely the night before I began having contractions. There was a well-known lady who presented television programmes and had been married for years but was struggling to conceive, and I prayed from the bottom of my heart for God to bless her, touch her and wipe away her tears; that night I felt his presence.

Over the following two days, I began having contractions before giving birth to our twins. Losing them was incredibly painful and I became very withdrawn, but within a month's time, I heard the happy news that the lady had in fact become pregnant.

However, not everybody was a well-wisher at this time and my friendship with Mrs Pyne was challenged by another lady in the church, from whom I sensed some jealousy. She manipulated us, telling Mrs Pyne that I blamed her for the loss of my twins, while at the same time calling me to ask if I had heard from or seen Mrs Pyne. She yoyoed between the two of us, sharing untruths about each of us to the other. Mrs Pyne and her husband grew increasingly quiet, and their visits began to wane.

This lady caused so much pain, so I decided to report the case to our pastor in the hope that he would be able to speak to Mrs Pyne on my behalf. He arranged for us to sit down together, and before long, the enormity of this lady's fabrications was evident. We realised she had positioned herself in the middle of our friendship and was fooling both myself and Mrs Pyne with her destructive tales. The pastor tried to persuade her to join the discussions, but up until now, we have still not heard from her.

Thankfully, the friendship between myself and Mrs Pyne survived the ordeal, and she gave me a beautiful item of jewellery when I left for Spain, which always reminds me of her. We cried tears of joy as she gave it to me, saying, "Angie, this is very expensive and I give it to you as a bond between us; no matter what happens, I still love you."

Calling my dad home

God hears our prayers, and while he sometimes gives us our heart's desire, he also knows when the time has come, teaching us to be patient in our faith. Nowhere was this truer than at the end of my dad's life. In 2003, not long after I married my husband, I was due to leave Tema to join him in Spain when I received a phone call to tell me that my dad was very ill. None of my siblings were with him as they were now all married, and the problems between them and my stepmum had led to Janet travelling to America. My dad was not happy that I was leaving, but he gave me his blessing, telling me to go to my husband.

I left on 14th February, and those who accompanied me to the airport to say goodbye told me how quiet and sad my dad was on the return journey. Once home, he remained indoors, barely venturing outside, and this continued until April, when he became seriously ill. Concerned for his well-being after he did not attend church one Sunday, a family friend knocked on my dad's door, calling his name. There was no response. Once inside, they discovered he had suffered a stroke and rushed him to hospital.

As soon as the news of his illness reached me in Spain, I prayed to God: "God, you know no one is living with my dad, and even if he survives and goes home, who is going to care for him? God please, let thy will be done. If you need to call him home peacefully, please do it, so he can avoid pain, suffering and shame." Lo and behold, God answered my prayers and called my dad peacefully home.

I was in Spain when arrangements were being made for his funeral. My family requested $500 to help make it a befitting service, but my husband did not have a good job at the time, so this was a lot of money for us. My siblings in Ghana were contributing less and I was eager to understand how the money was being spent and whether, since there were 15 of us, it was too much. However, once I saw the video of my father's funeral, I appreciated the extravagance of the occasion and I believe that if his spirit is somewhere, he will be very proud that we showed such respect.

Some of my siblings in Europe were able to go to my father's funeral, but I could not because I was pregnant with Deborah and had only arrived in Spain two months earlier. It was painful not to be there to say goodbye, especially given all the blessings he had shed on me, but I said a very beautiful prayer and wished him peace from the bottom of my heart. I am very proud of how well my siblings and family organised the event, clearly showing the world how much we loved our dad. My uncle told me that during the funeral, people mentioned me by my nickname, Mawulawoe (God will provide), and cried when they recounted how alone our dad was after I moved to Spain. I felt bad and very sad, as did my husband, who felt responsible for initiating my move abroad, but I reassured him that it was the will of God. I remain very thankful that my dad did not suffer from a prolonged illness and God was able to call him home peacefully.

A few years after the funeral, my uncle notified me of my inheritance, saying that the process had been amicable and the estate was being shared equally to make everyone happy. He said my dad had some shares in the bank, as well as some land and houses, which required me to return to Ghana to sign some documents. We flew back in 2006, along with our two-year-old, Deborah, visiting my dad's grave and leaving him some flowers while we were there. I am very grateful for how my family settled his estate and incredibly proud of my dad's hard work and the legacy he left. I wish for his soul to rest in perfect peace. Unfortunately, he never got to meet my children, but I remember how well he played with my siblings' children, and I know he would have loved them. The fact that they were born in Europe may have made my children even more extraordinary to him.

PART THREE

LIFE IN SPAIN

Chapter 11

A Fresh Start

I grew up believing that countries in Europe, such as the UK and Germany, superseded Spain in terms of significance, and it was not until I arrived in Madrid that I realised what a beautiful country it was and how loving its people.

We were greeted at the airport by my husband's Spanish friend Valdo, who drove us to La Mojonera in the province of Almería, where we first based ourselves. The journey took us past beautiful buildings dappled in light, and I felt like I was in heaven. I thought Spain would be like Africa, but it was different, and as we sped along, travelling through vast mountains, I could not believe its beauty.

La Mojonera

I thought I had said goodbye to my hardships in Africa, but I continued to face challenges at the start of my new life in Spain. The loss of my dad was enormous and shortly afterwards, we experienced a turbulent time financially. The joyful news of my pregnancy was swiftly followed by Alfred losing his job, and I remember wondering how we were going to cope.

Each month, we give 10 per cent of our earnings to our local church, a gesture in the Bible known as tithing, which provides food to help and bless people. I love paying tithe, but during that time, we received government benefits and once we had calculated the payments for our rent, car, food and heating, we were barely able to sustain ourselves on the remaining €20. We discussed the possibility of skipping tithe for a month, but I insisted that God would take care of us and suggested, "Let's challenge Him and see what happens?"

We paid tithe and went to church. In under a week, we had no money left. We went to the cashpoint to see if anything remained. Alfred put his card in the machine and discovered that €450 was available. We were shocked. "There is money in our account," he said. "Where has it come from?" We had no idea. My husband withdrew €100 and we went shopping. We waited for the bank to get in touch, but they never did, so we returned to the bank to collect the rest. To this day, we have no idea where the money came from, but we believe we saw the miraculous hands of God.

I always pay tithe; I think it is very important. This Christmas I paid it, and I said, "God, my birthday is coming, and I need money to celebrate you. I need customers to order cake." Lo and behold, business is good, and I have been getting continuous orders almost three or four times each month.

Deborah's arrival

By God's grace, I gave birth to Deborah Praise Nartey Amedeka on 20th January 2004, and the experience of delivering a baby in Spain was wonderful, totally different to Ghana. The doctors were lovely and caring, pampering me and making sure I was comfortable. They kept telling me, "You are so beautiful. Who did your hair?" They did everything they could to put me at ease and distract me from the pain. Deborah's birth was challenging as I was in labour for a few days, despite the doctors saying she was ready to come out. They would joke, "Don't worry, she's at the salon fixing her hair and make-up … she'll be out soon. "One brother from the church came to the hospital and sat in front of me singing, "The baby is coming; the baby is coming!"

Deborah was very fair, and her hair looked more like a white baby's, prompting the doctors to carry out tests to confirm she was ours, despite me telling them that my parents had fairer complexions. It took three days for them to be satisfied that she was ours, but they were very kind throughout, saying, "What a cute chocolate baby." Deborah was a bundle of joy who restored us after the loss of our twins.

Things started bouncing back.

Dangerous times for Deborah

My life with children was not easy and we nearly lost Deborah on several occasions. When she was about a year old, she was at home playing with her toys, among which was a plastic, battery-operated telephone. I was busy doing my chores when, unbeknown to me, she swallowed one of its batteries. It must have been in her stomach for a few days before, when changing her nappy, I noticed the colour of her poo was different, a bit black and yellow. The following day, all her poo was black, which made me very concerned. I called Alfred, who said we needed to act quickly. God told me to inspect the poo, which I did, with gloves, until I found the round, thin battery. I said, "Jesus!" and quickly reached for the toy telephone to understand how many batteries it held. There should have been two, one of which I had found in the poo, but the other was missing.

We took Deborah to hospital, where her tummy was scanned, but the missing battery was not visible. The doctors said the only means of being certain it was not there would be via a very risky operation. They told us to go home, pray and conduct a thorough search of our home before confirming the surgery. Lo and behold, God showed up in a loving way and we found the battery in a corner behind the sofa. We were so relieved. We updated the doctor, praise God, who said we were very lucky that the battery came out in Deborah's poo, otherwise, within two days, we could have lost her. They gave us medication to wash out her stomach and remove any poisonous residue from the battery, and we gave God the glory, for he always says we should not be afraid.

Many are the afflictions of the righteous one, but he will always deliver us.

Psalm 34:19

In 2007, my husband was invited to a programme in Barcelona at which the Ghana Union wanted him to officiate at an inauguration in Barcelona. As we drove to Barcelona on the motorway, Deborah, who was now three years old, suffered a convulsion in the car. I, sitting next to her, saw her eyes rolling and her teeth gnashing. "Oh my goodness," I cried out to Alfred, "something is happening to our baby," but Alfred could not stop or do anything to help. Our friend Paa Solo, a church member, who was in the car with us, tried to put a spoon in Deborah's mouth while we called the ambulance and exited the motorway into a filling station.

Deborah was given first aid treatment in the ambulance and taken to hospital, and I took myself to a nearby mountain where

I called out to God, "Please show up. This is the time I need you. I do not want to lose my baby." He saved Deborah at that bad time, and the experience reaffirmed to me that, "Greater is he that is in me, than the one that is in the world" (1 John 4:4). I knew that I was serving a powerful God, and no matter what the situation was, he would summon me and save me.

Deborah experienced another attack when the Very Reverend Bishop SN Mensah was staying at our house during one of his trips from Ghana. We moved her into our bedroom so he that could occupy hers, creating a bed for her next to ours. One morning, I woke up first and had a shower, while Alfred, who was recuperating from a night shift at work, slept. I returned to the room to get myself ready and heard the Holy Spirit saying, "Turn and look at your daughter again." I did, and I saw that she was very stiff and her eyes had gone. I screamed and woke Alfred saying, "Something is happening to our daughter."

The Bishop rushed in and prayed while we waited for the ambulance, and I saw God intervening. The Bible says, "He revealed to redeem" (Job 12:22), and it was clear to me that God saved Deborah through the presence of SN Mensar. If he had not visited us, Deborah would have been sleeping in her room alone and I might have found her too late. He was a blessing and a saviour, and his prayers healed her before the ambulance arrived to take her to hospital. I have been through so much and taken the pain, but God has been loving and showed up in many ways.

Fitting in

We worshipped alongside some lovely people at the church, and life went well until another drama came along. A woman in the church did not like me, despite pretending to, and several ensuing events made her feelings abundantly clear.

I was asked to host a group of missionaries from the UK after the Bishop recommended my culinary skills, but the woman was upset I had been asked because I was so new to the church. Nevertheless, I went to meet her so we could work on the missionaries' visit together, but any ideas I suggested, she disregarded. My husband came to pick me up and I asked if he could drop me at home as I was tired.

"How can you be tired?" the woman demanded. "What have you done all day?"

One of the missionaries overheard and challenged her: "You cannot say that. Angelina's been helping us; you need to appreciate her. She's tired and has a young baby."

Her dislike for me continued, and when she heard I was making a wedding dress for a spiritual daughter at the church, she interfered and called the bride five days before the big day to dissuade her from using me. She hated me for no more reason than that she saw my potential and wanted to bring me down. We had already made the bride's dress, the flower girl and maid of honour outfits, as well as decorating our car, so it is fortunate that my husband managed to encourage them to take the clothes.

By God's grace they accepted them, allowing us to make a few lastminute alterations to ensure everything was perfect. We went to the wedding, where everyone talked about the dress and told me how the woman continually found ways to insult me.

"I give God the glory," I replied. "I'm OK. It's up to her. When people say bad things about you and you do not hear it, they're only exposing themselves."

A victorious arrival

I begged my husband to find us a different place to worship, but he told me not to worry and to endure, and not long afterwards, we received news that he was to become a deacon. I was not happy as I had envisaged him becoming a pastor, but one faithful day, I heard a very loud voice say, "Tell Alfred to take another step." It was the signal we needed to leave the church and relocate.

Around this time, we were also trying to have more children, but sadly, I had two miscarriages in a row. We told our bishop, and he advised us to sleep on his bed without changing the sheets as he had anointed it. Shortly afterwards, I fell pregnant with our second daughter, who we named Victoria Korkor Nartey Amedeka, after the Bishop's wife, but also to mark her victorious arrival after so many miscarriages.

During my pregnancy with Victoria, there were a few complications, such as her being upside down in my womb, a problem that I was told would require surgery. My husband and I prayed for hours until our next scan appointment, when I told the nurse that God was going to perform a miracle. She looked at me, admiring my confidence, but by the next scan, we saw Victoria had returned to her normal position. The nurse could not believe it and said, "Wow, keep up your faith." Victoria is now such a lovely girl and we love her so much.

Called to Cuevas del Almanzora

We moved from La Mojonera to Cuevas del Almanzora, a small village with very nice people. I was looking for a job, a difficult undertaking because the children were still small, and so Alfred decided to open an African shop for me. We sold cosmetics and food items, and had telephones from which people could make long distance calls. It was the start of new things and life very quickly began to move on beautifully, with different nationalities using the shop – Senegalese, Spanish and Ecuadorians. We established a church with the wonderful Pastor Manolo, who was very kind to us, bringing us fine blazers, suits and shirts to sell at the shop.

All of a sudden, though, darkness descended on our lives again. During an economic crisis in Spain, when my husband was working in construction, the company was unable to pay him and his workers. We reached a point when we had no money and could not even afford to pay for our electricity; bills piled up until the electricity company came to cut the power. We had almost two years without lights, which was very difficult, especially with two small children, because everything had to be washed by hand. Deborah would remind me on the way back from the shop, "Have you got the candles?" We encouraged our daughters not to worry or feel bad for very soon we would have light again. Sometimes though, I would tell them there was a fault in the house so that they would not be scared.

It is very beautiful when you understand the workings of God, for when bad times come, you know how to face them. The Bible says, "He will not test us in anything that is beyond our strength" (1 Corinthians 10:13). Only a few people in Cuevas knew we did not have electricity, and we rejoiced in that moment, trusting God and knowing that there would be sunshine in our lives at some point. Those were the days I would pray: "Even though I'm in darkness, I know you're my light", and say my Beautiful Amen. From the outside, it was hard to see what we were going through as I always went to church smiling and, luckily, we had electricity at the shop, so I was able to iron our clothes there, or lie them under our bedsheets as we slept to straighten them out overnight.

These financial difficulties affected our marriage and left us unable to take care of our family here or in Ghana. My husband's mood deteriorated and he was very sensitive, getting angry over the smallest of things, but I didn't blame him.

Eventually, someone at the church told Pastor Manolo about our troubles and he said, "What! All this time you're going through this and you didn't tell me." Word spread and one day, a woman who knew Pastor Manolo called me over as I walked past her house to say, "We heard you've not had light for almost two years – is it true?" When I said that it was true, she replied, "You're a very powerful woman; not many people would be walking around smiling."

"What can I do?" I said. "We need to wait patiently for God to do his work."

A surprise visit from Pastor Manolo changed our fortunes. He rang the doorbell, holding out €3,000 for us, while insisting, "Take this money. I'm not taking it back from you. Pay whatever bills you need to settle and be at peace. I want you to be happy." I nearly cried and thought, "God, you're wonderful for using Pastor Manolo as an instrument to bless us." Wherever this man is right now, may God bless his very existence.

The week before, I had woken at dawn and cried while hoping for change. I found myself praying in a trance and I sensed someone tapping me and saying, "Look up. Can you see all those stars? Can you see that one particular star shining?"

"Yes, I can see it!" I replied.

"That's YOUR star," the person replied. I turned my back again and the person touching me had disappeared.

Then, I heard the voice again.

> Here I am to worship.
> Here I am to bow down.
> Here I am to say that you are my God.
> Altogether lovely.
> Altogether worldly.
> Altogether wonderful to me.

The song means a lot to me and every time I hear it, I am reminded of this dream sequence and the intense manifestation of God. From that time onwards, we were much happier, life began to move on, and we could see the sunshine.

A befitting funeral

I lost my mum in the twinkle of an eye; her death was completely unexpected and a big blow to me and the entire family. The reaction of my cousins and wider family in the days after she died was a real comfort and proved how much my mum was loved and cherished. I realise how integral she is to their story too, and what she meant to them.

It was a tumultuous time; Regina died within weeks of her sister AblaviDC Agbemabiawo, and they were interred together to save me the cost of two funerals. It was incredible because, in life, they had done everything together and it was as if they wanted to go to the grave together too. My cousins called from America and Ghana, wanting me to return home, but I had difficulties renewing my residency and did not have the correct documents to travel. In Africa, when parents die, children stand alongside the corpses and weep to feel remorse and show people that they are in mourning. However, if you are not there and there is no child, there is no spectacle or show of love and it can appear that the individual is alone and without children. I did not know how I would make it to the funeral, but my family and friends were so supportive, with Eric, a church member, offering to pay for my flights and help where possible. Our church in Spain also contributed to my mum's funeral costs and my return flights to Ghana.

My family did not give up, and, glory be to God, we saw our lawyers and were able to travel to Ghana with little Victoria, who was only one year old and Deborah, who was four years old. My cousins Antoinette and Kasuma, as well Uncle Baby, took care of everything, insisting that I should relax and not have too much responsibility. They bought the casket, dressed my mum (in the same clothes as theirs), and considered everything; I was completely overwhelmed. My mother-in-law also put in a huge amount of effort by preparing my clothes and plenty of food for the village before I arrived. All this work by others meant there was minimal effort for me to make, financially or otherwise, and showed how much they had adored Regina. She was buried at dawn, such was the custom, and my husband's family refused to accept any money, insisting their contribution should be seen as a mark of respect. I finally saw my mum and aunt lying together and I praised God for making it possible for me to see them one last time.

The Full Gospel Church in both Ghana and Spain was very supportive, showing incredible love during the loss of my beloved mum. However, returning to Spain proved challenging as I was told my legal documents were insufficient at the airport, requiring me to stay in Ghana until I received a new visa. I did not want to worry my family, so I did not tell anyone, and a whole month later, we flew back to Spain.

Our Eli arrives

My husband found a new job and things were running smoothly when I got pregnant with our little boy, Eli. The Spanish government had just introduced a new law providing €2,500 to every newborn child, which I thought was such a blessing. The favour of God began to locate us from all angles in various ways, and opened doors that had been closed in a similar way to when Joseph was thrown into a pit by his jealous brothers, who resented their father's favouritism, but he rose to become master of Egypt (Genesis 37). Life is a great teacher, and it has taught me so many lessons in which I have seen the goodness, power and love of God. Even if I had 10,000 tongues, I would not be able to provide enough praise.

My pregnancy with Eli was smooth and wonderful, his delivery beautiful but dramatic. I was in the shop when I felt the contractions and could not reach my husband, who was asleep after his night shift. I asked a brother from the church to wake him and tell him I was in trouble and needed to go to hospital, but the pain intensified, so I called a nearby shop to ask for their help, crawling along the pavement. They rushed out saying,

"Angelina, *¡Espera! ¡Tranquila!*" (Wait! Be calm!) before calling an ambulance. I was crying in pain when two of them arrived.

Alfred Eli Nartey Amedeka was delivered safely with the help of some very kind doctors at about 2pm on the afternoon of 28th April 2010, but nearly without my husband. He was oblivious to the action, woken only when a friend jumped through our neighbour's window and into our house. He managed to arrive just before Eli was born.

We had a massive christening for my son and things moved on very smoothly. I remember walking along the streets and being greeted by everyone as though we were public figures. Even the mayor stopped, which left a lot of people confused and curious as to who we truly were. It was all just the grace of God.

Time to move on

My husband received his Spanish nationality in 2013, but we began to consider relocating as life in Spain was increasingly challenging. We thought about Germany and Canada, but decided the UK would be the best place, especially for the children.

Alfred contacted a few friends to get a sense of their lifestyles and to enquire about work as a lorry driver before deciding to visit London ahead of the move. He called me from the hotel he was staying in to discuss how expensive everything was before being advised by a friend to travel to Birmingham where things were more affordable. He immediately saw the difference between the two cities and began looking for accommodation for us in order to prepare for our arrival.

Back in Spain, I sold the goods from the shop and wound up our lease, as well as getting myself and the children organised for the move. I travelled to Ghana again, before returning to Spain to celebrate our 11th wedding anniversary and my 40th birthday. It felt like a time of celebration as we also had a farewell party to which we invited many friends, combining it with Victoria's 7th birthday party. We shipped most of our belongings such as the fridge and bed to the UK in 2015 instead of buying them again, and Alfred bought our flight tickets.

We were ready to go.

PART FOUR

LIFE IN THE UK

Chapter 12

Birmingham Beckons

I thought the children might be frightened on the journey to the UK, having never been on a plane before, but they were so excited and kept calling, *"¡Que chulo!"* (Cool!). My husband had bought a small dark green VW Polo with which he picked us up from the airport. Eli, four years old at this point, walked over to the car saying, "Is this your car, or somebody else's?" His face changed and he was not happy; this car was like our Spanish car! It was autumn and the girls, who were very observant, looked out of the windows, asking questions and remarking at how everything looked so dirty. Eli joined them, saying, "I don't like anything here, even my dad's car! I don't like the colour." We had no peace and they complained nonstop, but we kept saying to ourselves, "It's just the weather; when they get there, they'll like it."

However, as soon as we arrived at our new home in the UK, Eli dropped his bag containing his Real Madrid skating shoes on the floor and said, "Where am I going to skate?" Our house in Spain was bigger and once the corridor doors were open, there was ample room to skate. We all laughed, especially when he opened the cupboard doors and saw there was no food in them. "I hate the UK," he said. "There's nothing here." Everything felt smaller to him, and the weather was colder, but once we showed him the big garden, he was happy, and now he loves the UK and would never want to leave.

I will never forget one particular drive home from church when the children were small and heavy rain had caused a large puddle of water to block a main road on our route. I did not have much driving experience and I felt a little scared and anxious, but Deborah came to the rescue and found another way home on Google Maps. Unfortunately, however, we took a wrong turn and found ourselves on the motorway, the children screaming, "*A donde vamos*?" (where are we going?). I do not know how we managed it, but, thanks to God, we got home safely, our journey home not a 15-minute drive but an epic 2-hour adventure!

All three of our children have done so well in their education and their Spanish roots have shone through, with both Deborah and Victoria achieving A*s in their Spanish GCSEs. Deborah is studying law in Manchester, Victoria is in Year 11 at Ormiston Sandwell Academy, preparing for her GCSEs in June before starting sixth form, and Eli is in Year 9.

Our daughters Deborah and Victoria play the piano in church and Eli plays the drums. I like to say, "Mummy sings and Daddy preaches the word of God." Our children are God-fearing, respectful and obedient, and their lifestyle has positively influenced so many children. Once, at Victoria's birthday party, her best friends Alexie and Janell gave a speech in which they said, "Victoria has really transformed our lives for the better." We have taught our children how to show compassion and because of this, they always think of others and put their feelings first. They know how to be firm in times of trouble and how to keep their faith in God when they face challenges.

Chapter 13

Helping Others

People often comment on how happy I appear and ask for my help, which has led me to take up a mentoring role in my community, with an emphasis on marriage counselling. It all started when my husband and I arrived in the UK and noticed how many people were getting divorced. Feeling that something needed to be done, I formed a marriage group called the Purpose Driven Group in 2015, which had the slogan 'Love is Sweet' (*odoye dee*), to help motivate the ladies around me. One of its policies is, 'say no to divorce', and we work hard to teach people that nobody is perfect in this life, and that we must learn from one another.

The Purpose Driven Group

The group started in our house with just five families, and by the grace of God, 8 years later, we have expanded to 30 members, with 27 kids. The group is strong and healthy, full of love and unity, and we support one another in various ways, especially when it comes to celebration; we learn to celebrate people while they are alive. Teamwork and the love of God is the bond that keeps us strong.

In 2016, the Purpose Driven Group hosted a barbecue at our house to celebrate the first year of being together and it was a largely pleasant experience.

It was also a group member's birthday, so we cut a cake for him as we celebrated.

We hired a bouncy castle, which the children loved, with some of them sleeping over and jumping straight onto it again the next morning. They were really sad when it was deflated, but at least we all had fun. We celebrated the second anniversary in Edenton which was also fabulous, with lots of invitees.

We cover interesting topics such as helping people understand their spouses better by analysing different temperaments and tendencies. Based on theories from Ancient Greek and Roman physicians and philosophers, we look at the four main humours or characteristics in human beings: the choleric, the phlegmatic, the melancholic and the sanguine. Every one of us exhibits a little of each; for example, I am primarily phlegmatic but also a little sanguine. I am creative and I cook and bake, while my phlegmatic side makes me very calm and a bit slow; I take my time when I do things and I make sure I do them properly. Major problems can arise if, for example, your spouse's nature is choleric – if he is the hot type – and yours is much calmer, more phlegmatic. He or she might be strident, have little patience and go beyond the limits of what is acceptable when upset, but if you are aware of this and are a man or a woman with a tender heart, you will know how to handle them and there will always be peace. These opposites can create problems in marriages, especially because, as African people, we do not learn about these things, which can lead us to judge people wrongly. If, however, you know the character of a person, you can find ways to support one another.

It is rightly said that it does not matter where you go in your life; what matters most is who you have by your side.

I would like to reflect on our first president and his wife, Mr and Mrs Ohene, who played a fantastic role during their tenure.

Fast-forward a few years and we have handed the presidency baton to Mr and Mrs Kwabia. Sister Phyllis is doing a wonderful job, her leadership has really pushed us forwards and I am proud of her as the mother of the group.

Life coaching

When we lived in Spain, I used this awareness and understanding in a social setting with a lady who was a hot type and always had problems with people, but she respected me, and if I gave her advice, she would take it. Even now, in the UK, she always thanks me for being there and giving so much to her life; she is now into the Church as well.

In my family, I have a relative who is also a hot type and people in the family are scared to get close to him, but he likes me so much. When we were younger, he would visit my shop in Ghana, we would have fun together and he would ask for my help to find a girlfriend. He found a wife and is now in his 60s, but if I ever go to the village, he keeps asking, "Where is Angela?" People do not understand why he likes me so much and I do not know why; it is the grace of God.

Our counselling group also helps our children understand their rich African heritage, how it sits within their UK-based upbringing and how to balance each side of themselves. It can be difficult, especially for those children born in the UK, when their parents try to give them an authentic taste of Africa, maybe offering foods that are so different to what they eat when they are with their friends. We openly discuss these issues, not to confuse the children, but to reassure them and help them understand these cultural complexities.

I have first-hand experience of imparting African values to my children and understand how differently it sits with some of their peers. Our children would come home and tell us how their friends were in relationships at 16 years old, while we advised them not to hang around with boys until they were, at the very least, over 18 years old, when we felt it would be more acceptable. In Ghana, we were told to wait until we reached a certain age and then a man could come after us, unlike the Muslim faith, in which children are married young. When I was growing up, you would not even dare to kiss someone outside, such was the expectation from, and respect for, our parents and older generations. Nowadays, however, social media is changing people's mindsets and you can see that the youth do not care in the same way we did.

In our house, we try to blend the two cultures where we can as our children will visit Africa and need to understand where they are from and how each culture behaves. They always say they are Spanish, but we remind them they have Ghanaian blood in them, and they need to learn the language, and how to eat the food and respect their elders. In Ghana, you must greet any elderly person you pass in the street and offer to help carry their belongings, saying "Mum (or Dad), can I help you?" If anybody has a heavy load, you must relieve them of some bags, ask them to sit down, check they are comfortable, and get them a drink before they carry on with their tasks. My husband's time in Europe certainly gave him a more relaxed approach. Shortly after our marriage, he was being affectionate as we queued at a Ghanaian bank when a security man said, "You do not do this here, can't you see there are children? You need to respect others and yourselves." Alfred did not see the problem of it, but it shows the very different mindsets. He once gave me a peck on the cheek while we were walking in town and a Ghanaian woman saw us and said, "Oh, you are still doing this at your age? Why are you doing it in public? We are from Africa." Afterwards, my husband said, "Wow!"

Lady pastor

I am a Christian and a lady pastor at the Full Gospel Church International, where my husband is the Reverend minister, and we work together for the Lord. In Spain, we ran the Full Gospel Church International, which was funded by us when our daughter Deborah was two years old. This involved quite a bit of travel with her while she was young as she accompanied us on visits to the new church. We now run the Birmingham branch, which was also funded by us, here in Oldbury.

The Catholic Youth Organisation I went to in Ghana is very close to my heart, and I have a friend here in Birmingham called Veronica who attended the same CYO and who I met again miraculously in Smethwick after we had not seen each other for years. I had no idea she lived in the UK and had no information about her whereabouts, but we met in a chance encounter when I dropped a church friend called Peace back at her house, not knowing that she was a mutual friend of Veronica's. As I moved my car, Veronica arrived, saw me and could hardly believe her eyes. She beeped her horn, reversed back and said "No ... no!"

I looked at her and said, "You look familiar too."

Veronica started reminding me of our childhood memories, of Celestina and of her father. I jumped out of my car, and as I hugged her, we both felt very emotional. Since then, we have become close friends again. Sometimes, she sends me pictures of our Ghanaian friends, and she has reconnected me to an old CYO friend called Comfort.

There is something about Peace's house because, miraculously, I also met my own cousin there, a woman I did not know from Adam.

When Peace opened her front door, I saw a lady sitting inside the house and greeted her in a general Ghanaian dialect. "Why are you talking like that?" Peace asked me. "She speaks your language." I asked where she was from and she mentioned Tegbi, the exact village my mum gave birth to me! In short, Bridget's grandad is the brother of my grandma, making her my cousin.

I have a cousin called Moses in Bedford who knows more about our family, so I called him immediately and put him and Bridget in touch. After a while, he said, "Do you know you're sitting right in front of your own family, your own blood sister?" Bridget came to the UK to study law, and she finished her master's before studying for a PhD in Northampton. She is now a parliamentary judge in Ghana. Shortly after discovering this connection, my cousin left Bedford, picked her up in his car and they all came to my house, where I cooked for them.

This world is something else! We called our family in Ghana, and they were so happy to hear about all their relatives coming together. Miracles follow me around and this was one of the happiest moments in my life.

Nurturing my children

Children are a precious gift from God, made in His image. God wants us to take good care of them, to treat them with love and value them as part of His image. As parents, we are our children's stewards during their earthly life. The Book of Proverbs instructs parents to "Train up a child in the way he should go" so that "when he is old, he will not depart from it" (Proverbs 22:6). My husband and I try to make God the centre of our home by fortifying our children's faith in Christ.

The Bible says children should obey their parents, and likewise, parents should be mindful not to be overly harsh (Ephesians 6:4). Children do what we do, not what we say. They imitate our behaviour and everything we do, whether it is good or bad, and we must set a good example for them to follow. The way we talk to people, to our spouses, our way of dressing and the kind of food we eat, it all matters. We have taught our children how to show love and kindness to people by giving willingly from the heart. As we prepared for my 50th birthday celebrations, I took my son Eli to look for a venue, and we visited a beautiful place called The Conference Suite in West Bromwich. I watched Eli taking videos as he exclaimed, "Waooo … waooo …

Mummy, you deserve this place." However, the price of the venue put me off and I explained to him that we needed to either look somewhere else or go home.

"Mummy," Eli said as we got into the car, "don't worry, I'll help you pay for the venue."

I looked at him with a smile and asked, "Do you know how much we're talking about here?"

"Mummy, I've saved £70," he said, "so I'll give you £50 and keep £20."

I was overwhelmed and felt so blessed to have such a wonderful and caring 13-year-old boy, who will take care of us when we grow old.

My children view me as a strong woman when it comes to challenges, and I always try to equip them with hope and empower them when things are not going well. Deborah was harassed at school after refusing to join a local gang, and the experience left her very upset and wanting to change schools.

Her hair was pulled and her appearance insulted, but one day, an attack was reported to the headmistress, who told the police and drove Deborah home. I told Deborah she was a beautiful black girl who needed to stand up to the bullies and reminded her of the song I'm no longer a slave to fear because I am a child of God. My encouragement had a real impact, and shortly afterwards, she asked to sing the song in church while playing the piano in order to glorify God. She told the congregation how my words motivated her to not be a slave to the bullies.

One awful day, Eli was run over by a car; I nearly collapsed when I received the news. I drove like a mad woman to the hospital, listening to Premier Christian Radio, and I heard God speaking to me through Psalm 46:1. God bless Eva and her love for my son, she rushed to the hospital before any member of the family. At the hospital with Eli, we encouraged him by playing music such as *God will work it out* and *If it had not been for the Lord by my side*. I remember how much these songs touched one of the nurses, who started sharing her testimony with me. Jesus Christ Himself suffered and faced tribulations and said, "In this world you will have trouble. But take heart! I have overcome the world" (John 16:33).

On Alfred's 50th birthday, we thanked God for saving Eli from the hands of the enemy and we turned our mourning into dancing, as advised in the Bible (Psalm 30:11). In our parenting we have always made God bigger than our problems, and God proved himself to be mighty by saving Eli's life, ensuring he made a good recovery and was able to walk normally again. The enemy intended to bring evil, but God was there to make it good. Halleluiah! I am grateful to Hall Green Secondary School, from the headmistress to my coworkers, for their concern and support during Eli's accident. We were also supported tremendously by people's prayers, notably, those of the Purpose Driven Group and the entire Full Gospel Church International.

Raising children is a great responsibility, especially when you include the task of blending African and European cultures. Thank God our children are responsible, intelligent and hardworking. They help with most of the house chores, we cook together, have fun together, and go on holidays as a family. We are fortunate and blessed to have them as a bundle of our joy, and we could not be prouder.

A misunderstood gift

One day in Ghana, giving got me into trouble. I had been keeping a close eye on a young girl in my Sunday school group and her appearance suggested she lacked some sort of care. During a conversation, she told me the woman she lived with was not her biological mother and her story touched me. I decided to buy her some clothes and I also asked my sister, whose daughter was the same age, if she could contribute some items for this little girl. The next time we were at church, I gave them to her, but the following weekend, her guardian tried to attack me, accusing me of criticising her capabilities. I apologised, explaining that I only ever intended my gift to be a goodwill gesture to bless the child.

I was very upset when she returned the clothes, and I returned home, crying. I asked God why I was paying such a price for showing goodness and love, but instead of the incident tarnishing my outlook, I followed the words of the Bible and continued to do good. It was a reminder that the enemy is always close by and despite our suffering, absolutely nothing should separate us from God. People will always want to quench our light, but we must stand still and embrace every situation, whether painful or not, and continue with our journey.

Chapter 14

A Passion for Food

I love the kitchen; it is the centrepiece of my two main hobbies, cooking and baking. It is my office, and if you told me to sleep in the kitchen, I would. My husband sometimes comes into the kitchen and says, "Go upstairs and go and sit down," but I do not like sitting down. I adore places where there are stoves and ovens, which is why the food technology department at Hall Green Secondary School, where I work, is perfect. I am also a supply teacher specialising in cooking and baking. I love my job with all my heart; it is my passion.

I love creating, and when people give me the design for a cake, I always try to add details that will make it stand out more; I enjoy trying to do something new in everything I do. In Spain, my friends would always comment on how regularly I redesigned and moved items around in our house, especially in the living room.

Life is like a recipe: sometimes you weigh everything accurately and use the correct ingredients, but you still do not get the result you deserve. However, God always finds a way, even when it seems impossible. I have been a baker for a few years now, but one particular day I will never forget. Someone had ordered a velvet cake, for which I followed the recipe, achieving a quality bake, but during the decoration, something terrible happened. Upon adding each layer, I realised the whole cake was falling and I let out a scream. The cake needed to be ready for the next day at 12:30pm, so this was a disaster and a nightmare. I had to restart the cake from scratch, and I did not think I would meet my target. Despite everything, I successfully baked and designed a cake more beautiful than I could have imagined.

Everything works out for those who love the Lord, and it is worth remembering that whatever comes easily does not last. The weight of your battle carries the weight of your victory.

Qualifications

Life in the UK offers much more in terms of education and job opportunities. When I first arrived, my mentor encouraged me to do an adult education course and become a cooking teacher. At first, I was reluctant because I thought, owing to my experience as a Sunday school teacher, that I belonged in a children's setting, but I took her advice and I do not regret it. Once my online studies were complete, I accepted a role at Deborah's secondary school in the food technology department before moving to a different school, where I was promoted relatively quickly.

People complained that I had it too easy and that it was too soon for me to be fully employed, but despite receiving this hate, the Lord was with me. In the end, I moved to the adult education centre, where I did my online courses and where the staff were lovely and respectful. Their courses lasted six weeks and for two years I rotated among different groups, which gave me the chance to teach lots of students. Sadly, a lack of funding curtailed my contract, and I began to feel negative about my future career.

However, God was faithful again and one day, a man (who I did not know) called John phoned me. He said he had seen my CV somewhere and the only thing I was missing was a degree, which I should try to do. I said, "Do you know my age? Do you know who you are talking to? I'm a pastor's wife, with so many responsibilities, I don't think I can focus or study." He kept pushing, saying there were no limits on education in the UK and he encouraged me to meet him at one of Birmingham's universities. A lady from the church accompanied me, but when we got there, they had no record of the man, I thought, "Is he an angel or what?"

I decided to listen and approach the University College Birmingham, but enrolment had closed; however, a few hours later, I was asked to return with my qualifications. I checked that Alfred was happy for me to go to university and he said it was fine if I felt I could do it. The next day, the university called when I was in Sainsbury's to offer me a place, which was like a dream come true. The course was challenging to begin with as I had not been to school for a long time and everything was new, but they were very encouraging.

A robe and a certificate

In 2021, I graduated with a degree in baking and patisserie technology – I call it an old lady's degree! I also completed Level 3 diplomas in baking and cake decorating, cooking and nutrition, winemaking and weight-loss training, as well as juice and blending skills with Global Edulink in Birmingham on 8th August 2019.

I was very excited about my graduation party and my husband postponed a trip to Ghana in order to attend. However, the Devil insisted on making things hard for us, and before I knew it,

Alfred had contracted Covid. We were very upset but, if all went well, he would be able to finish his quarantine on time for the graduation ceremony. As the crucial date grew closer, his condition deteriorated, and before I knew it, both Victoria and Eli were also infected, leaving only myself and Deborah symptom free.

Deborah took great precautions not to catch Covid too, wearing masks and gloves and spraying the house with disinfectant, but in the end, she did go down with it. I was devastated, but God was by my side and the silver lining was that even though my whole house was struck down with Covid, I did not catch it. Despite cooking for them and monitoring their temperatures, I remained safe and healthy.

By my graduation day, Alfred's condition was so bad that, through tears and with the help of a local pastor, I called an ambulance. The paramedics confirmed that my husband was free of Covid and that he would improve soon, and thankfully, Eli and Victoria were well enough to accompany me to the ceremony.

It was a day of mixed emotions; on the one hand, I was happy to be graduating, but on the other hand, I was heartbroken that not all my family could be there. Receiving my certificate in a robe was a once-ina- lifetime experience and sadly, Deborah and my husband were unable to witness it. However, the Lord is my strength, and I was able to graduate graciously, and although I was not in the mood to celebrate, my friends decorated the venue, and all my children were able to come to the party.

I requested a steadfast love song to be played during my entrance in honour of Alfred, who was still in hospital, and

Deborah told me that as I walked in, she burst into tears. The event was successful, and it was beautiful to feel the love and support of the Purpose Driven Group and pastors from other parts of the country, as well as my extended family. The next day, Alfred was discharged from Sandwell Hospital, by God's grace.

Hall Green Secondary School

I began working at Hall Green Secondary School in September 2021, where I met wonderful and amazing coworkers who were very supportive and caring. I immediately felt at home and have really enjoyed working with all the staff, especially Mr Phansi, Trevor and Petrona. I love the time we have together at lunchtime, cooking healthy food such as vegetable soup, salad, Spanish omelette, curry and roti. We also hold Bible discussions and pray as a family of God, with unity and love.

The main gospel music anthems we play are *God will work it out* and *All my life you have been faithful.* These songs are our main source of strength and reflect our experiences of God's faithfulness. Petrona and I share many testimonies about the goodness of God, and I see her not just as a colleague, but as a sister, advocate and supporter. I am grateful to have her in my life and feel incredibly fortunate and blessed to be part of the Hall Green Secondary School team.

Clap for the carers

I would like to use this opportunity to thank the NHS for all they did during Covid and all that they continue to do. The compassion they have for each life is remarkable. Doctors cure us with medicine, but nurses cure us with hope, care and compassion.

I remember calling our GP when I was sick and I met a wonderful nurse called Anita whose professionalism filled me with so much hope, and I healed with no medication. I walked out strong and happy, finding her compassion and kindness more powerful than any other medicine.

Nurses deserve to be celebrated every day because nobody can comprehend what it takes to be in harm's way and yet be strong enough still to love and care for people. Yes, they get paid for their job, but no money can ever buy heartfelt empathy or a genuine feeling of compassion and care. The job of a nurse is really tough, especially during the era of a pandemic.

Similarly, the role of police officers in any society deserves appreciation. Police officers are available for the safety and security of the public at all times, risking their lives to protect our lives and belongings. A policeman saved my live once at a Sainsbury's filling station in Oldbury, when a man attacked me for no reason. The officer appeared from nowhere, professional and compassionate, checking I was OK before allowing me to drive away peacefully, feeling safe and secure. I am extremely proud of the police for the fantastic job they do all around the world.

MY
PHOTOGRAPHS

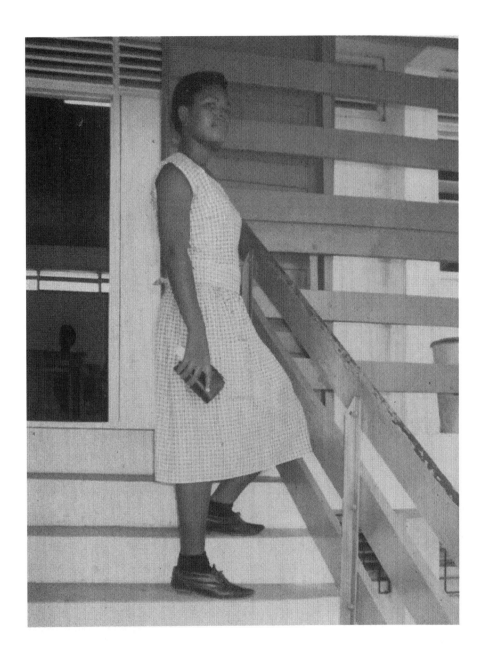

144

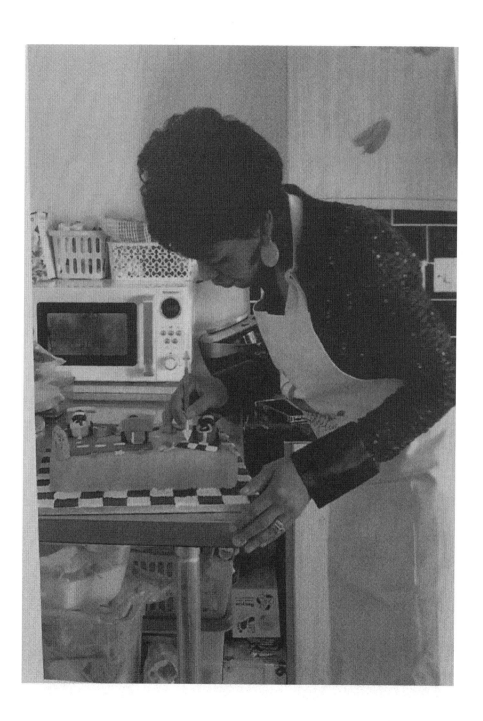

My Children's Blessings

Mama, Mama … where do I begin? As I grew older, all I did was realise and admire just how strong you are. All you ever wanted for us was nothing but the very best. I've learnt so much from you, Mama; I pray that God continues to bless you with more strength and grace for the rest of your life. I love you.

Deborah

My mum is my biggest inspiration and I really look up to her. I love many things about her and one of the many is her ability to smile and stay positive, even if she's going through a hard time. I've experienced my mum going through many hardships, but every time, she continues to put her pain aside to smile and be happy for me and my siblings. My mum is always there for me and helps me even when she has problems of her own, and I'll forever be grateful for what she has done for me. I really thank God for such a great mother.

Victoria

My mom was and is the most important and favourite person in my life. She never fails to care about me. She is always the person to take care of me when I'm ill. Even when I caught the Covid, she fed me with her bare hands. When she's down I always hug her and try my best to cheer her up. I did, I do, and I will love her the most.

Eli

Reflections

You are not who people say you are, you are who God says you are. It does not matter how many people hate you; God's love is enough. Fighting a battle in silence does not mean you are weak, rather, it is preparation for the victory.

The weight of your problem is the weight of your victory.

Do not let your negative thoughts have the final say in your life. Think positive. *Greater Is He That Is in Me* than any surrounding problems.

Do not let negative thoughts have the final say in your life. Remember, God opens doors for us; it is our choice to go into the wrong entrance.

Challenges come to test your personality and quality.

Life is not a competition, but you can win if you put in a little more effort.

Storms are very strong and mighty, but you can calm them with *A Beautiful Amen*.

Sometimes difficulties are not there to destroy us, but to help us see our full potential. You are the driver of your life, so do not let anyone take your seat. Great and mighty things never happen in your comfort zone.

Life is like a transport system which many people board from different junctions and alight at various destination. People will come and go, and even your own shadow will leave you in your dark moments.

Words are powerful, and whenever we speak, they come to fruition. If all hope seems lost, try a different approach in order to be yourself.

Our fingers are not equal in length, but when you bend them, they align; life is easier if we understand individual differences and adjust accordingly.

You may not feel recognised where you are at the moment, but favour will locate you and announce your success, if only you recognise yourself.

Watch the actions of the people who say they love you, not their words.

Epilogue

Life is not a competition, it is timing, and when you put in a little effort, you will always win. Regardless of gender, or who we are, we should not belittle ourselves because God has a plan and can use us to do so many things. We need to remain positive and not let any negative thoughts have the final say in our lives. Words are powerful, and what we say to ourselves will ultimately come through.

Some of the things I have been through should have defeated me. The trauma and the loss could have taken me, but I am still strong – I have not allowed the sour situations to defeat me. God lifted me when I was down and has been my strength when I have been weak, protecting me and my family from so many dangers.

God promised He would go before us and level every mountain, and *even though I walk through the valley of death, I will fear no evil.* The Lord is my strength and my salvation. Whom shall I be afraid of? Even in times of famine, He has been my provider. I have never seen the righteous begging for money. God will satisfy us with a long life.

My Beautiful Amen signifies that there will always be a way out of life's challenges. It is important to accept and embrace adversity, safe in the knowledge that God is a constant source of strength whose power we must learn to trust and rely upon.

Family Tree

Grandfather	Abraham Besah Gbeve Amedeka
Grandmother	Madam Rebecca Abenorlawobu
Dad	Alfred Amedeka
Grandfather	Mr Dzowyorwui Agbemabiawo
Grandmother	Madam Sexovor Galedzi Kokoroko
Mum	Regina Atsufi Agbemabiawo
Stepmum	Janet Amoafo
Stepbrother	Richard Amedeka
Brother	Mr Franklin Astigui Akpalu (now lives in the US)
Author	Angelina Amedeka Agbemabiawo
Spouse	Alfred Nartey Accam
Children	Deborah Praise Nartey Amedeka
	Victoria Korkor Nartey Amedeka
	Alfred Eli Nartey Amedeka

Timeline

1925	Dad, Alfred Amedeka, born in Weta, Ghana, passes away April 2003
	Attends elementary school and college; studies marketing at university. Lecturer at university in Accra
1933	Mum, Regina Atsufi Agbemabiawo, born 20th July in Keta hospital, passes away 22nd June 2008
1943–1950	Regina attends Roman Catholic school, Renown Teachers. Attends vocational school in Keta, Ghana, graduated to be a vocational teacher
	Relocates to Accra, to join big sister to trade.
1973	Angelina Amedeka, born in July in Keta, Ghana
1979	Angelina moves to Tema to start school. Moves to a private school, Compresco School Academy
1983	Angelina attends middle school
1993	Angelina leaves middle school and sets up dressmaking business
1999	Angelina opens boutique called Community One
2002	Angelina marries Alfred Nartey Accam
2003 (April)	Dad, Alfred Amedeka, dies in Tema, Ghana, aged 78
2003	Angelina and Alfred move to Almería, Spain

2004	First child, Deborah Praise Nartey Amedeka, born
2007	Second child, Victoria Korjor Nartey Amedeka, born
2010	Third child, Alfred Eli Nartey Amedeka, born – referred to as Eli
2015	31st March, Angelina moves to UK

Printed in Great Britain
by Amazon

49470935R00095